Hear Our Voice One Israel

Standing Up for Judea, Samaria and Jerusalem

HOWARD TEICH

HEAR OUR VOICE ONE ISRAEL
Standing Up for Judea, Samaria and Jerusalem
By Howard Teich

Inquiries, Comments and Participation: hearourvoice.com
Judea and Samaria Website: www.hearourvoiceisrael.org
Howard Teich Website: www.howardteichny.com
E-Mail: HearOurVoiceHT@aol.com

ISBN: 0692898905
ISBN 13: 9780692898901

CONTENTS

INTRODUCTION

I stood at Shiloh overlooking the Jordan Valley and the Jordan River, looking into Jordan itself, and in the distance, I saw Mount Nebo, where God had stood with Moses pointing to Canaan, the Promised Land for the Jewish people. I realized that my Southern view was of Jerusalem and the Dead Sea. At that moment, I felt the extraordinary spirituality of this place, the religious capital of the ancient Kingdom of Israel, and the place where the tabernacle once resided.

I was on the lands of Judea and Samaria, with Hebron, Shechem, Ariel, and numerous significant sites that are part of our Jewish heritage, each with its own history, and each with its own stories to tell. So, take a moment, and just imagine these sights and the history, and their significance! And now as I had experienced on another visit to Israel, imagine you are standing on the Judean Mountains in Judea and Samaria looking East, with an unimpaired panoramic view of central Israel – first Ben Gurion Airport, then Tel Aviv and the Mediterranean Sea only miles away – and recognize the clear, apparent danger to Israel if it were not in Israel's control.

The world calls upon Israel to "give it back" in the name of peace, to a Palestinian Arab people who do not have the long-term claim to the land that the Jewish people have, who have refused land-for-peace offers, and though they forge their own truths, many in the world still buy into their narrative.

Too many forget that since the Six Day War of 1967, Israel has sacrificed for peace the entire Sinai to Egypt; walked away from Gaza for the promise of peace, with quite the opposite happening; removed its troops from Southern Lebanon for peace, and Hezbollah moved in with its thousands of missiles; withdrew from part of the Golan to have a cold peace with Syria. And, just to put this in perspective, Jordan relinquished any claim it had for Judea and Samaria ("its West Bank") to the control of Israel.

In giving back the entirety of Sinai to Egypt for peace, Israel had to evacuate 50% of the land area of the expanded Israel, with oil reserves and strategic importance for training of its military and air force, among other things. Israel had to tear down every remnant of Yamit, a most memorable bloc of Israeli Sinai settlements I had visited on a mission – its buildings, synagogues, greenhouses with flowers, removing all its children and its future, all of Yamit in the name of peace – turning it back into barren desert. And let's not forget Israel even had to leave its tourist areas of Sharm El Sheikh and Taba in the Southern Sinai, every last inch of them that they had developed in Sinai.

In giving Gaza to the Palestinian Arabs in the name of peace, Israel had to remove the residents of Gush Katif from their beautiful forty-year-old communities, including every building, every synagogue, every Jewish child and person, and even every grave (yes, even the bodies of the non-living). The only things left intact were those items requested such as greenhouses, and yet, the Palestinian Arabs destroyed them because they had been built by Israel, and from their perspective were Jewish greenhouses. And as we now know, Gush Katif once deserted by Israel, became a terrorist strong hold, with thousands of missiles and armed troops that have been turned against Israel.

Israel's wars have been defensive and for survival, and deals to end the wars were pragmatic and/or based on countering outside pressures. Under United Nations Resolution 242, the idea of giving back extensive land in Judea and Samaria was certainly never mandated nor intended. With the Oslo Accords, allocations of Jewish and Palestinian territory were made, as were principles such as demilitarized Palestinian zones and local ruling authority, and separations between the two peoples, and yet the Accords have deteriorated in effectiveness.

The Torah tells us that this was the land that God brought us to, the home of Abraham, Isaac, Jacob, Sarah, Joseph, Rachel, Rebecca, Leah, where our great Kings David, Solomon, Samuel, Ezra ruled, and essentially where our Twelve Tribes lived. Within the oft-proposed two-state solution ostensibly to preserve Israel's Jewish, democratic character and create a Palestinian State, the Palestinian Arabs' proposals for peace have included the removal of all 500,000 Jewish pioneers in Judea and Samaria along with their cities and communities built over the last 50 years or more. And, we may well imagine that our archeological sites, our history on the land would be obliterated, and this land would become a new, dangerous front for missiles aimed at Israel.

Here's how I see it: the establishment of the State of Israel 75 years ago was a monumental achievement for the Jewish people, and its success was foreseen by Herzl, Weizmann, Jabotinsky, Ben-Gurion, Meir and others to give our Jewish people a homeland for the Jewish people to be able to live in safety. The completion for us was the retaking of Judea, Samaria and Jerusalem, our spirit, our soul and homeland that God gave us. With this unification, we as a Jewish people can be what we were intended to be. So, I say we must never leave it.

I am proud and fortunate to be an American, a New Yorker, and Jewish. Although I have been immersed in Jewish community affairs and organizations for many years, starting with my early years as the New York Chair of Israel Bonds' New Leadership division, I am not a Torah scholar, nor am I an Orthodox Jew. Throughout my life I have been a member of Conservative synagogues and a long-time involved Democrat invested in social justice causes, and though I have been called by some people a so-called "right-wing" advocate for the State of Israel, I myself see myself as a leading voice for an emerging "new mainstream".

I published this book to make a more compelling case for this new reality. In the articles that I have written over the years and that appear in this book, I cover a wide range of thinking, and you can approach reading them in year order, or by topic. It will work either way. I have placed my most recent five articles first so you would start with my most current thinking, and then the others are organized chronologically with their own significance and relevance.

This book is for Israelis and Jews in the Diaspora, Christians and other non-Jews, and for all people in the world, for this decision and outcome, impacts us all. We cannot remain silent, we must stand up and be committed and counted, and the world must Hear our Voice: One Israel! I have spoken up on this topic over the years on many occasions, and I am available for speaking engagements and debates, as we must engage more people in the significance of creating One Israel.

SPECIAL NOTE: I could not complete this Introduction without acknowledging, and thanking Jerry Lippman, publisher/owner of the Long Island Jewish World Group of Newspapers, who published most of these articles, and assisted in editing them. His role has been invaluable!

THIS IS NOT A FAIRY TALE. WE ARE CARRYING THE TORCH OF OUR PEOPLE!

January 2023

There are times that prove to be transitions, turning points. Such is the time we are in. And it involves multiple issues in America and in Israel. I am most concerned here with the American Jewish community – whether we are meeting the challenges of our times and whether we are prepared for them.

I have the sense that today's American Jewish community does not either know its history, nor take seriously how fortunate it is to have the State of Israel and a mostly protected Diaspora community in the 21st Century. Although we just celebrated Hanukkah, I believe few realize that our celebration of Judah Maccabee's victories was on what is today Judea and Samaria (the West Bank) – which is the **central** target of the Boycott, Divestment, and Sanctions(BDS) movement. What hypocrisy for those who refuse to recognize the reality of our history!

The BDS movement was established in 2005 originally by the Palestinian Arabs with the hope of isolating our Jewish state,

Israel, in order to destroy it. Today, joined by others, BDS has caused the cancellation of speakers and conferences on campuses across America, student confrontations, boycotts of Israel products, and even restrictions on discussions in some synagogues. It has brought fear, helped increase anti-Semitism across America, and allowed anti-Semites such as Kanye West to voice their bigotry in words, scrawls and deeds.

J-Street, B'Tselem, Americans for Peace Now, and other so-called pro-Israel organizations call our ancestral homeland of Judea and Samaria "occupied land," referring to Israel's occupation of Arab Palestinian land, and I say "hogwash." It *is* time we as a Jewish community get strong, fight the fight that needs to have leadership, and gain the education needed to refute the false narratives thrown against us.

How sad it was during Hanukkah to hear Jewish leaders agreeing that Hanukkah today is celebrated by Jews as an answer to Christmas. How sad it was to hear some leadership say it is not an important holiday, or a holiday to celebrate that one vial of oil lasted eight days.

How sad it was to see leaders overjoyed at a photo-op lighting a public menorah and yet not carry the most important message of our people – that Judah Maccabee was a great Jewish hero. He stood up to the Greek overlords when no one else would in order to retain our homeland in battles near Beit-El, Modi'in, Ayalon Valley, Shechem, Beit Heron Ascent, before then entering proudly into Jerusalem and our Second Temple. He carried the torch of our people for his generation, that was in 165 BCE. His stand was in the land of today's Judea and Samaria.

Israel's newly elected government led by Prime Minister Benjamin "Bibi" Netanyahu, has assumed leadership at a time of opportunity and danger, and needs the support of the entire

Jewish community. Although democratically elected by the people of Israel, many of us in the non-Orthodox community who have been on the front-line of progressive politics may have concerns about some of its ideological positions. We have every right to speak out on them, as they are related to the very essence of who we are as a Jewish people, and yes as Americans.

Yet, when it comes to the history and security of the Jewish people and Israel, we have a responsibility that supersedes our individual biases. The continuity and welfare of our Jewish people come first. Hillel said it best, "If I will not be for myself, who will be for me?" Those in the Jewish community who adamantly have positioned themselves against Israel's reclaiming our homeland of Judea, Samaria and all of Jerusalem in 1967 are not carrying the torch of our people, and I can only shout out to them the words of a contemporary Hanukkah song, "Don't let the light go out." Your positioning is harming Israel and the Jewish people.

Last month, we commemorated the 50th Anniversary of the death of one our most legendary thinkers of modern times, Rabbi Abraham Joshua Heschel. I have reached a time in life that, as an active participant in the Jewish community, I am continually searching for the light. I celebrate Rabbi Heschel for his faith in God and humanity, that we are all brothers and sisters here, that the Prophets need be heeded, that tikkun olam (repair of the world) is needed, and that Israel is an integral part of our future. And we must learn from spiritual leaders such as Rabbi Heschel. It is not a time to be silent!

I quote Rabbi Heschel here from a Rabbinical Assembly lecture he delivered soon after the Six-Day War as recorded in the book, *Spiritual Radical* by Edward Kaplan, as it has great significance for all our consideration, "Unprecedented. A people despised, persecuted, scattered to corners of the earth as though dust, has the audacity to dream regaining authenticity, of being free in the Holy Land…There is a covenant, an engagement of the people to the land. We could not betray our pledge or discard our promise."

In my book, ***Hear Our Voice One Israel: Standing Up for Judea, Samaria and Jerusalem,*** I present a solid case for the importance of this land to Israel and the Jewish people. In short, aside from its history as our Biblical land (which is at the top of my list), I recognize the strategic imperative of having the Jordan Valley and safeguarding the border with Jordan. I value the commitment of so many pioneers who have gone to the mountaintops to build new communities where ancient ones existed, and to bring a devastated forgotten land to life. And I recognize the need for having a solid relationship with the neighboring Palestinian Arabs who live here.

Perhaps our age now could be viewed as a prophetic time as we look to new opportunities to expand the Jewish homeland that God promised us. Israel was the first part, and now we need to officially reclaim – whether through sovereignty or annexation – the land of Judea, Samaria and Jerusalem that is sacred to us, and that we now control. And as now advocated by Haim Katz in the new Israel government, with whom I fully agree, we must increase tourism into Judea and Samaria. On that note, it is well past time that our American Jewish organizations take their missions over the Green Line – not only to Ramallah to meet with the Palestinian Arab leaders as has been the custom of too many of them – but also to cities, communities, homes of the Jewish pioneers who now live there, and to businesses and institutions such as Ariel University that now has in excess of 15,000 students. The world need see the miracle of the rebirth of Judea and Samaria first-hand, and at the same time it would add to its economic development.

We must confront our positioning in the world at large, and that will take a certain genius of its own. Recently, Israel made great strides to expanding economic opportunities and tourism, and bringing closer the days of peace for Israel in the region through the Abraham Accords (a series of joint normalization statements between Israel and United Arab Emirates, Morocco, and Bahrain). Recently Rabbi Or Rose of Hebrew College in an article dedicated to, *Fire and Light, Anti-Semitism and the Celebration of Jewish Life,* , wrote, "As we attempt to respond to the current surge in anti-Semitism, let us follow in the footsteps of Heschel and other brave and inspired leaders, working to extinguish scorching flames of hatred and increase the radiant light of Jewish wisdom and innovation."

The narrative of the Jewish community in America and throughout the world must not become anti-Semitism nor victimhood, for that is not who we are as a people. We must bring the boldness, the courage and the optimism of a Judah Maccabee to our actions now. Think of who we are, a Jewish people with Israel as our living homeland after a 2,000-year absence and yearning, and a strong, vibrant community in the diaspora with a still golden age in America. America was a refuge for our ancestors from persecution throughout the world in the years before Israel, with the hope and reality of freedom and opportunity that remains with us today.

We need explore, recognize, and relearn our 5,000-year journey as a people, for since that first burning bush at which Moses spoke to God, we as a people have always brought light out of darkness, in carrying out our service to God on Earth. That's our quest, and our destiny as a Jewish people, for our soul is guided from that path. That was the message of our Prophets Amos and Isaiah, heroes Ruth and Esther, patriarchs Abraham and Isaac, leaders such as King David and Joshua, and more contemporary legends such as Rebbe Menachem Schneerson of Chabad Lubavitch movement, Heschel and Israel Prime Ministers David Ben Gurion and Golda Meir.

It has not been an easy path, and that is what has been set out for us. Too many in our Jewish community today do not know nor respect our history and our spiritual essence. That's what is missing, for us to portray ourselves as a unified community so powerful that the truth would be our truth, not someone else's falsehoods. And we must find that unity as we face a world in which our very principles are often under attack – and too often from within our own Jewish community. That's the crushing part. Perhaps it is reminiscent of historical divisions in our history that have often brought us down, and we need to make sure we do not repeat our mistakes.

Let me share some thoughts from my experience with the Native American community. I learned of their ultimate respect for the sacred, their land, their people, and their spirituality. It has no doubt influenced my current thinking. As a Jewish people, we are not only still around after thousands of years, we are thriving – still lighting candles in the tradition of our *people,* bringing light to the world, and we have our spiritual homeland. I look at the people who cause outrage with an increasing number of anti-Semitic incidents. They cannot impact us, for they are merely a blemish to our human spirit.

As an American, I think of President John F. Kennedy's 1963 "Peace Speech" at American University, in which he sets out a path that we need reminding of today, "Peace... does not require that each man love his neighbor, it requires only that they live together in mutual tolerance, submitting their disputes to a just and peaceful settlement. And history teaches us that enmities between nations, as between individuals, do not last forever. However fixed our likes and dislikes may seem, the tide of time and events will often bring surprising changes in the relations between nations and neighbors. So let us persevere."

This is not a fairy tale, it is profound, and it is our journey learned during our years in the desert carrying us into tomorrow's leadership. We are carrying the torch of our people, and we must increase its brightness in our generation to glow forever for everyone. We must never let it go out.

ISRAEL MUST DEFEND ITS FUTURE: PALESTINIAN MARCH ON BORDER IS NOT PEACEFUL

April 2018

No country need accept a terror organization threatening to disrupt their future. Gaza's Hamas, backed by Iran it appears, claims that it is marching to Jerusalem to take back a country and land that was never theirs.

Its mission is to get inside Israel. It is not to peacefully protest on its side of the border. It is to cross the border, destroy the security fence, and invade the Land of Israel. Those are the facts on the ground. And Israel has the responsibility to safeguard its citizens and protect its country like any other country would do, and should, do.

When I saw the movie, *The Darkest Hour*, telling the story of Winston Churchill and his courage in facing the WWII enemies when he took over the British leadership from Neville Chamberlain, I immediately thought of Israel today. Certainly, this is not the darkest hour for Israel, in fact I could make the case that it is one of the brightest periods, yet it is a time that we all must stand by Prime Minister Netanyahu and his decisive leadership that has solidified and protected the future of Israel. He is no Chamberlain.

And yet the world criticizes Israel for protecting its future. This Gaza insurrection is tantamount to an attempted invasion. Tens of thousands of Israeli citizens are in nearby towns, protected only by the security fence and the Israel Defense Forces(IDF) from these highly intentioned Hamas terrorists. And whatever force is necessary to protect Israeli citizens from the actions of outside enemy troops cannot and should not be considered from the point of view that they may have been overly harsh, that it is disproportionate. Israel has given the warnings that it will be tough this time, and the people in Gaza have their choice.

So, let's really start to clarify the game being played out on the ground. Yes, I said enemy troops. The Gazan, Iran-backed terrorists may not be clothed in traditional military uniforms, but make no mistake, they are military troops. And in their current actions, they have prepared for battle, and entered into battle. It is not a peaceful rally when known radical terrorists, openly enemies of Israel, mix themselves in with women and children, knowing that they are creating a clearly dangerous, yes, a potentially tragic situation. In fact, it is hardly civilized that Hamas puts women and children on the frontlines, and that is what really needs to be investigated, and called out by the world.

This so-called "March to Return" began on March 30th, and was announced by the Gazans to be a six-week protest for the right of return of the descendants of the Palestinian people who left their land in 1948, and scheduled to end on May 15 with their return to Jerusalem. It is reported that Hamas will pay the families of anyone killed $3,000, and lesser amounts for those injured. Hamas has strategically set up tents for the terrorists and their allied participants along the 40 mile stretch of the border.

This is no peaceful demonstration, and yet the automatic reaction included the Secretary-General of the United Nations Antonio Guterres calling for an independent investigation of Israel's response, and Kuwait bringing a draft resolution before the UN Security Council on the night of the first Passover Seder, Shabbat evening, that an investigation proceed. Although Israel would not betray the holiday and appear, the United States, to our great credit, blocked the resolution, and US Ambassador Nikki Haley once again stood up for Israel, and for true justice.

The draft resolution called for Israel to respect "international human rights law and humanitarian law including protection of civilians" and called on the Israelis to show restraint to prevent further escalation. It was reported that the Palestinian Authority in Ramallah launched an attack on Ambassador Haley, attacking her as an "Ambassador of animosity, hatred and dark ideology." We must ask: where was the world-wide call for the Gazans to respect the security of an independent country, Israel?

After years of listening to the insidious public relations attacks of the Palestinians, and trying to "sheepishly" defend Israel, it is time we called things as they are. NO, we need not "sheepishly" defend Israel. We need applaud Israel and speak truth to power.

When the Palestinians reportedly made a statement that the "massacre carried out by Israel occupation forces against defenseless civilians during the peaceful Anniversary of Land Day," we need to call them on their lies and misrepresentations, not apologetically but forcefully and angrily. They have the choice. Israel has reportedly indicated that every person that comes close to the fence risks their lives. So, Hamas need pay attention this time.

Israel on its own left Gaza, pulled out their citizens from Gush Katif, destroying beautiful Jewish communities, to leave Gaza for the Palestinians, to create the opportunity for a peaceful transition on that land. Instead of developing the possibilities of the land and its beaches, Hamas and the Palestinian Authority established in Gaza a terrorist center that has not spent its money on improving its people's well-being nor establishing the potential of Gaza as a future Palestinian gem with a growing economy and potential tourist mecca.

It has created an infrastructure to maintain their goal of the destruction of Israel, holding its people back even to the extent of keeping their citizens in substandard UNRWA refugee camps to make the case that their people remain displaced from their homes.

In that time, Israel has had to defend itself against thousands of missiles launched against the people of Israel by Hamas, sheltering their neighboring cities and villages. I even had to run for shelter from one of those missiles at the end of the last Gaza War, so I know it is real. Israel was diplomatically and verbally attacked by many countries and people for these wars, and I ask the question for the world to answer: does not Israel, and the Jewish people, have a right to defend their own country, and live in peace? If not, then the world best have a solid rationale for their thinking, and I have no doubt that I will not be happy with its thinking.

Realize that Gaza is now one prong on a multi-front aggressive strategy to take over and destroy Israel. This is an open conversation of Israel's enemy neighbors, backed by an Iranian regime that looks to the day that the destruction is real. Israel has fought against a Hamas radical terrorist organization that hides behind their civilians, many good people, women and children, who are under their control and at their mercy, and deserve better in their lifetimes.

Israel and many of its Arab neighbors now are finding common ground, the potential for a bright future that will enhance the lives of all their people. The possibilities are unlimited if this path is followed. No more excuses for those who breed evil, no more appeasement for enemies to a future world of peace. And no more Chamberlains who do not act forcefully for what is right and good. The time is now to call out Hamas, Hezbollah, and their terrorist cohorts for whom and what they are, and how they are treating their people.

So, the world does have to take action, and it should start now. Israel must defend its future, and the world need stand with them. We can create a better world for future generations, one of love and togetherness, not of hate and war. We must end the lies of Israel's enemies, and that starts by telling the truth of this Hamas insurrection at the Israel border.

THANKS TO TRUMP ONE YEAR LATER: PRESIDENT HAS KEPT HIS PROMISES

January 2018

Just over a year ago, I wrote an article, *"A Most Optimistic Time for Israel: The Trump Era Bodes Well for the Jewish State."* It's a good time to look back and look forward. Nothing like seeing where you are on the path, and who is there with you, and who, and what, are the obstacles in the way. It means really avoiding the clatter and seeing the reality. That's one of the reasons I have always separated my politics from my positions on Israel.

Oprah Winfrey said at the Golden Globe Awards the other night, "what I know for sure is that speaking your truth is the most powerful tool we all have." And she said it in the context of our trying to "navigate these complicated times." So, here's my truth.

The Trump Administration has created an atmosphere for Israel that has not been seen in a United States Administration for many years. It starts at the top, and that is President Donald Trump, and he has kept his word. Statements of US Ambassador to the United Nations Nikki Haley have been nothing short of extraordinary, and most noteworthy. Certainly it was expected that US Ambassador to Israel David Friedman and son-in-law Jared Kushner would be supportive, and they have been.

And I have only seen Vice President Michael Pence once in person, and it was at the CUFI Conference a few months ago in Washington DC. So, here's how I described the experience to myself right after the Conference, "When the Vice-President attended and gave a keynote speech at this Conference, speaking out on the Administration's support and friendship to Israel, on their commitment to move the American embassy to Jerusalem, not if but when, and the alignment and understanding of key issues was apparent, you know this Administration really does have Israel's back.".

Let's start at the top.

President Trump made a stop at the Western Wall during his visit to Israel in late May, 2017, his first foreign trip abroad, and just a few months into his Presidency. No other sitting President had visited this holy site of our Jewish people, as it is considered controversial by some as still seen as part of the so-called "occupied territory". However, he clearly recognized its spiritual significance to the Jewish people, respected that Jewish connection, and by his visit, trampled on those who do not consider the Western Wall, The Temple Mount and Jerusalem as part of our Jewish history, and as part of Israel. A most memorable, and meaningful event for the Jewish people.

Then, in December 2017, President Trump recognized Jerusalem as the capital of Israel, and the process for moving the United States Embassy to Jerusalem has begun. In 1995, Congress enacted legislation with strong bipartisan support that would have had the United States Embassy moved from Tel Aviv to Jerusalem by 1999. At the time, it was strongly opposed by the White House, and so, it was constructed in such a way that the President would have the power to suspend the move for six months indefinitely. Each President since then had used the waiver to avoid the move, and that has now changed.

It is interesting to note that the reaction to this action worldwide was less severe than expected, and yet not a surprise that the majority of countries in the world would vote against the United States recognizing Jerusalem as the capital of Israel in a United Nations vote. Some disappointments came in surprising places and applause to Togo, Marshall Islands, Nauru, Micronesia, Palau, Honduras and Guatemala for standing with the United States and Israel. Without naming them, it is noteworthy reviewing the 35 countries that abstained from the vote, a positive sign.

The Palestinian reaction was relatively minimal, notwithstanding that they went to the United Nations for the vote, had minor skirmishes against Israel, and made a statement that the United States could no longer be involved in the so-called peace negotiation. In fact, there has not been a peace process for years. And that's the truth, the Palestinians walked away from it. President Trump did emphasize, though, that this pronouncement would not affect any decision made between the parties in a final peace agreement.

Some organizations and political figures voiced their opposition to the move, criticizing the timing among other things. Let's be clear, though, they would never find the right timing. And it is most interesting that some of those who spoke against President Trump's move had actually voted for the act in Congress that he now signed, and they now condemn him for acting upon it. Jerusalem is the heartbeat of the Jewish people, and has been for the past thousands of years. The saying goes, from Psalms 137:5, "If I forget you, O Jerusalem, May my right hand forget its skills."

And it is nearly unforgivable that some so-called Jewish leaders spoke against this recognition.

So, let's continue.

President Trump has taken a harder line towards the Palestinians expecting them to step up to the plate for peace if they have any interest in it. His most recent action threatened action is to cut funding to the Palestinians in an amount over $300 million, as he sees no interest on the part of the Palestinians in moving the peace process ahead, and therefore does not see the money now spent on UNRWA as essential.

President Trump announced that the United States was withdrawing on December 31, 2017 from UNESCO after their continued anti-Israel bias in their decision-making, the latest in July, 2017 when UNESCO passed an outrageous resolution to consider Hebron and the Tomb of the Patriarchs as endangered Heritage sites of the Palestinian State. That followed a resolution the year earlier in which UNESCO adopted a resolution which questioned Israel's ties to the Western Wall, and, in essence nullified the Jewish people's ties to the Temple Mount, saying that it is sacred to the Muslims and calling it only by its Muslim name, Al-Aqsa Mosque and Harim al-Sharif.

President Trump has recognized that the enemies of Israel are making a world-wide effort to delegitimize Israel, and in the process strip our Jewish people's history. So, he has spoken out against it. The Boycott, Divestment, and Sanction (BDS) Movement has had limited impact, yet wide visibility which is harmful to Israel. As an example, when entertainers go to Israel and perform under a cloud of threats, we must let them know our appreciation, and when others fold, and cancel their tours, they should also hear from us, our disappointment and anger. Boycotting Israel has been around for a long time, and this is no time to cave.

So, here are some truths as I see them.

In this multicultural world, Israel is seen by many as a pariah country, formed by the colonial powers out of the Ottoman Empire after World War I, the Balfour Declaration and the enactment by the League of Nations. Some say it was guilt after the Holocaust that created the atmosphere for the United Nations vote that gave Israel its independence. I say it was the spirit of the Jewish people, from 2,000 years ago through Herzl and so many others, and the willingness to put their lives on the line for this Jewish State that resulted in today's Israel.

I can easily understand the antipathy of many of the Arabs towards Israel, though I may not like it. The religions are different, perhaps conflicting in part, and the Jewish people in some strange way remain a threat to the ongoing vision of Islam, and the Muslim people, though for many years we lived together in friendship. Fortunately, better understanding is growing once again, and I would certainly welcome the day when we are all looking out at the world through a common vision of respect, and peace. Jordan and Egypt did that decades ago, peace was declared, and they are models for the future.

Although we have built bridges with many people, only recently am I recognizing the inherent threat of the last remaining issues in a peaceful future for Israel. I am thrilled that in Judea and Samaria we have our land in our possession again, and that as time continues, and archeological digs move forward, and the land is studied, there is more and more proof that this is the Biblical land of the Jewish people. I am excited that Jewish pioneers have settled on that land, as the original pioneers did in Israel, and made deserts bloom, and we see today in Judea and Samaria, wines of the olden days, flourishing on the same land, and in some cases through extraordinary technology, with the same grapes as 2,000 years ago.

Yet, for some, that is perhaps the threat. For many in the

European Union who oppose Israel's settlements in Judea and Samaria, it is this new dynamism that may well be the threat to their thinking. As secularists, they looked to a secular Israel. They do not want to see the land of the Bible flourishing again. They do not want to see proof that the Biblical history has truth. So, as the development of the historic land of Israel and Judea and Samaria continues, there is more fear of holding onto their positions, which become weaker as the truth of the land becomes more self-evident.

And I remember the days when the early pioneers went into Judea and Samaria, and many were Ultra-Orthodox Jews from New York, from Brooklyn, and you could see, and feel the invectives of many secularist and non-Orthodox Jews who wanted Israel to give that land away rather than it attract a more Orthodox population who would flourish on the land and become an increasingly significant part of the population of Israel. That's a truth of my memory.

And today, we face something that is almost odd, it has become cool, and the in-thing to stand up for the Palestinian people, and stand against the Israelis, particularly among the more so-called liberal and youth crowd in America, particularly on its campuses. And we have not countered it well, notwithstanding that Israel has fought to have a Homeland for its Jewish people in the center of these vast Arab lands. Israel is an enlightened, modern society that more and more is carrying out the vision of our Jewish people, being a light unto the world.

I can no longer understand how members of the American Jewish community are willing to put Israel in a situation where its security and future is totally at risk. That's what the 1967 borders, the Green Line would do, and there is just no question about it any longer. The two-state solution as we knew it is history. So, I would call on all of those well-meaning people to take a new look, and stop being so oppositional. Israel can be Jewish and democratic, just look at the facts today.

So, let this be a time of common understanding for the Jewish community. There's a window right now in terms of the opportunity for the future of Israel, and the Jewish community need be unified. I remember during the early days of the Clinton-Gore Administration, when the opportunity seemed so large for movement in directions that many of us wanted, we had the sense that the President can make it happen on his own. It's not true. The popular support makes the difference.

Those who may differ on issues of significant importance to us, such as the right of women and men to pray together at a certain location of the Western Wall, let's agree to put that on public hold for now, and enter into internal discussions on that within the family. Yes, stand your ground on issues that are important to so many of us in America, and yet stand with Israel. Jewish organizations such as Jewish Voice for Peace, B'Tselem, New Israel Fund, Breaking the Silence, J Street and others are problematic, for they sell themselves as pro-Israel, and yet they undercut world support for Israel. There is no place for them at the table.

Additionally, it is a sad commentary that today's American Jewish community has a decreasing importance to Israel. Israel is part of the world community, and although the American Jewish community has become one the greatest civilizations in the history of the Jewish people, and we are fully flourishing, we no longer have the leadership under a consensus concept of leadership that makes a world-changing difference to Israel. Fortunately, we have many who have been outspoken for Israel over the years, and yet we are no longer unified for Israel, and we are not one voice in support of Israel.

Israeli's Naftali Bennett gave us some insight to Israeli thinking at the 2014 Sabin Forum in Washington, DC, saying, "Modern Zionism was all about creating a shelter for the Jews... it was a secular approach that had the audacity to change history. But one hundred years on…the reason we are in Israel is not because it is a shelter. It's our Homeland. I want every Israeli child to know our history."

And let me add this most important paragraph. I want every American Jewish child to know the history of our American Jewish community, as well, as it is extraordinary what we have accomplished in freedom. We have stood up for social justice, we have stood together with people of all backgrounds and colors, and shouted out for their rights, and we have created some of the most significant leaders in this country in government, in the arts, in science and industry far surpassing our wildest dreams. And we have been an enlightened, committed people.

We are different than Israel, like any members of a family, and we all come from one common thread, with a common history, and celebrating our holidays together, with an interest in business, and in leading interpretations of our Torah and Midrashim. And Israel should pay more attention to us and learn from us. Together, we will be able to shine that light out on to the world, and we will well be able to face the dangers of people and countries in this world who still find reason to hold on to hatred of the Jewish people.

The message is out, though, the American Administration is no longer leading from behind. We need not look through the eyes of other nations to understand why our perceptions and interests may be different than theirs. We do not need their agreement. We need to be standing tall and telling the truth. This Administration is doing that with Israel.

And this is the time for we American Jews, whatever our differences, to stand together in an unbreakable bond with Israel as it negotiates its future status. It's a tough world, and it's so significant to have America with Israel. Notwithstanding other policy differences, we must let President Trump know we appreciate his support for Israel.

A MOST OPTIMISTIC TIME FOR ISRAEL: THE TRUMP ERA BODES WELL FOR THE JEWISH STATE

December 2016

The Republican National Committee Platform referred to Israel as an exceptional country, a bastion of liberty. In its language, it removed the call for a two-state solution, sending that choice back to Israel and its neighbors. It called Jerusalem the eternal and indivisible capital of the Jewish State, and it no longer condemned settlement development.

Seeing these words, one can imagine a great and optimistic future for Israel, an opportunity to move along an enlightened agenda for our Jewish Community and for Israel, one that we have not seen as a possibility for many years. And I say that can happen if we stand with newly elected President Donald Trump, and with the Republican Congress, on Israel. Let's commit to making that happen now.

Yes, it is a hope, perhaps a dream, and not a promise nor a done deal. Nothing is. And I know I will have mystified many of my friends and colleagues with that thought. After all, I am a Democrat and supported Hillary, and yet from the Conventions on, it became more and more clear to me that the election of Donald Trump with a Republican Congress would best serve Israel. And, that's what we have.

Jerusalem is the capital of Israel, declared by Israel in 1950, and yet that has not been universally accepted, not even here in the United States of America. I want to throw out a best hope, right up front, yes, a request of, and challenge for President-Elect Trump and for the Jewish community in America. President after president have committed to moving the United States Embassy to Jerusalem, recognizing Jerusalem as the capital of Israel, and yet once they are elected President they go back on their word. Although the 104th Congress enacted the Jerusalem Embassy Act of 1995 to move the American Embassy in Israel to Jerusalem by 1999, and it has been sent to each President since then, none have signed off on it, each taking a six-month waiver provision.

My hope, my dream would be that President-elect Trump would sign off on the move of the United States Embassy to Jerusalem in his first hundred days, and that we celebrate this extraordinary event in May 2017, the 50th Anniversary of the reunification of Jerusalem. It should happen, and certainly would be part of the new thinking in Washington DC, and we cannot expect it to happen without our support in the hinterland. We know we can no longer count on our mainstream Jewish organizations for such actions. That's why a group of us have started to organize an effort to stand with President Trump in getting this done.

Why such hopes, and such dreams? Clearly, President-elect Trump, his history and family are key to this, adding in the Republican Platform on Israel, and the control of the Congress by the Republicans who have been firm friends of Israel for many

HEAR OUR VOICE: ONE ISRAEL 3 years now, both in their words and deeds. The time is just right. So, I continue my wish list.

I welcome the indication from the Trump people that they will not be looking at settlements in the same way as previous Administrations, for that is our future. This false issue has been raised as an obstacle to peace for years now. There is plenty of land for everyone, and I say the Jewish community has every right to be on the land of Judea and Samaria, its homeland. And as we know, even if it were suggested that peace was on the horizon with the Palestinian Arabs requiring some rearrangement of the settlements, certainly by Israel's previous actions that could be done, although I would oppose it. Simply put, settlements are not, nor ever were, an obstacle to peace.

For over a decade, I have called for a declaration of sovereignty, or the annexation of Judea and Samaria, and I have not been alone in this, although many in our community have fully opposed this possibility for peace. Recently I was interviewed by Rabbi Mark Golub on JBSTV, and he asked me the question, how as a centrist-liberal Democrat could I have my position on Judea and Samaria – that it was not consistent. I answered that it was 100% consistent, particularly when you consider a Palestinian Arab demand for peace that no Jews remain in Judea and Samaria. You see I reject the reality that a Jew should be limited from living anywhere, just as in America, long ago our U.S. Supreme Court rejected the possibility that someone should not be able to purchase a house in a certain neighborhood, among other reasons, because of the color of their skin, or their religion.

Many of today's so-called Jewish leaders are opposed to my views, and I would hope that as we move beyond the Obama Era and into the Trump Era, their significance wanes. The shadow of people like George Soros, and the group of puppets that he has controlled in undercutting real pro-Israel sentiment in America, will now have to accept a new, brighter future. I would expect that the influence of organizations like J-Street and its self-proclaimed Jewish leader will be on the decline, as the light shines again.

And what a perfect time of year to have the Trump Administration prepare to govern in America, as we celebrate the Festival of Lights, Hanukkah. Last year I wrote of the miracles of Hanukkah that we celebrate during this wonderful Festival, and that I saw it as not just a celebration of the Maccabees and the duration of the oil burning, rather as a celebration of our continuing miracles and the victories of our Jewish people in our extraordinary history, and the light that we bring to ourselves and to the world. I envision three groupings of candles when I look at the Menorah this year.

We light the first candles for all that have come before our time. We remember and celebrate Judah Maccabee leading a rebel army, the Maccabees, to retake control of Judea for the Jewish people in 164 BCE, creating the Hasmonean Dynasty that ruled until 63 BCE. He restored the Jewish religion to its position in the land, rebuilding the Temple in Jerusalem, and in a miracle that we remember forever, found one vial of oil that lasted eight days, restoring the eternal flame to the Temple.

We light the second grouping of candles for that which has happened in our time. Recently, I was in the Metropolitan Museum in NYC, and it is celebrating the Hanukkah Season with the display of an extraordinary Silver Menorah from Lvov/ Lembourg, Poland, approximately 1866-72. My father's family lived there at that time, so the Menorah had additional and special meaning to me for perhaps my family had seen this Menorah lit in its time and place. And I took note of its inscription from Psalms 3610, "With you is the fountain of life; by your light so we see light."

A miracle of our time was our survival from the Holocaust, and the continuing growth of the Jewish people in Diaspora. And a most extraordinary miracle of our time has been the creation of the State of Israel, and its development over the past seventy years, a dream in the late 19th Century, a reality in the mid -20th Century, and a work in process taking us into the 21st Century and beyond. So, we light the second grouping of candles on the Menorah for the miracles of our time.

And what light do I see this year from lighting the other candles! It is the world taking note that there is a change, a world acknowledging and recognizing the new positioning of Israel. It has built a closer, more meaningful relationship with Russia, China, and some of the Arab, Muslim and African countries. Israel has economic and military strength, and significant cutting-edge breakthroughs in new technology, both in hi-tech, agriculture, water, and energy resources. And Israel has a culture and people learning, and taking its place in the world.

In the years ahead, with the One Israel I dream of, and the annexation of Judea and Samaria that I advocate for, I see a country that finally can move towards an Israel being secure and becoming a true light unto the world. Without the constant disruptions, and terrorist threats by the Palestinians, I can see a true path for the Jewish people as well as a general uplifting of the Palestinian people's quality of life, and recognition by them that they can be partners in Israel. And so, I see a bright future for Israel in the world community.

I see the opportunity for an extraordinary archeological exploration of Judea and Samaria in the years ahead, such that we can fully confirm, or interpret the stories of our people, as told in the Torah, or in our oral history. And as we move further ahead, both Jews and Arab Palestinians living together again in Judea and, as they did for many centuries, peace becomes more real, and the opportunities for all the people living in the land improves significantly. I can see a renewed spiritual revival for Israel, and one that they bring to the world.

And it is the hope that in lighting these final few candles, we have a renewed enlightenment of the American Jewish community, as well, a recognition that our soul comes from Torah, and our commitment to our people, its history and its laws, as well as tikkun olam, our service to all other peoples. We are an astonishing people in America, one of a handful of our most extraordinary civilizations in the history of our people. Freedom has served us well. Out of our current great divide, though, it's time we found common ground again, and I see that in the shining light of the final candles in the Menorah this year, when we all stand together in unity with Israel.

With the lighting of the final candle, I look out to our future, the 100th Anniversary of the Modern State of Israel in 2048. Then, for the Jewish community, the story of their 3,000-year history in this land of Israel has truly come to life during the 2040s, as excavations near Shechem, Shiloh, Hebron, Jerusalem, the Galilee and other places have continued to uncover the Biblical stories of our people. The techniques that were used in these architectural digs have been shared with Israel's Arab neighbors, and ancient stories will have come to life, bringing tourists to all of Israel's and its neighbor's land, and bringing a cooperative venture in new wealth to all countries in this region.

I see that our dreams of today have become tomorrow's reality. This beautiful land of One Israel, stretching from the Mediterranean Sea to the Jordan River, I see with peace internally and with its neighbors. And I see hundreds of thousands gathering in Jerusalem, Jews, Arabs, and Christians together, to celebrate centennial of Israel. The people of the region will have found their shared history and set aside the age-old fights that kept them divided. Through joint ventures, new sources of water and energy will have been explored and developed that have become models for the world at large. With a population of Jews in Israel now exceeding 10 million people, the worldwide population of the Jewish people finally has exceeded pre-Holocaust levels, with over 19 million Jews in the world in 2048.

I see this Trump Era as one that makes us see more clearly again, and although I may have gotten ahead of today's reality, it continues my optimism for the future. It's my hope, and vision! We must stand strongly for the restoration of our entire Homeland, and I do think the time is right for it.

HYPOCRITES ALL: WHAT DOES IT MEAN TO BE PRO-ISRAEL IN 2016?

August 2016

First Lady Michele Obama, in her first-night Convention speech, delivered the thought that should make us all recognize the significance of having our Jewish people in Judea and Samaria, as she said, "I wake up every morning in a house that was built by slaves. And I watch my daughters – two beautiful, intelligent black young women – play with the dog on the White House lawn."

I say the same, in another place, and in another way, and with another timeframe. I wake up every morning knowing that my people were slaves in Ancient Egypt, and were led to the Land of Palestine, to have it as their home. Though exiled for 2,000 years, and suffering innumerable untold travesties including the Holocaust where six million were killed, we never gave up hope and determination, we prayed, and today my Jewish people are back in our homeland, the Land of Israel including Judea and Samaria and the undivided, eternal City of Jerusalem.

In the Book of the Prophet Amos, in the words of God, it

is said, "I will restore my People Israel, They Shall rebuild ruined cities and inhabit them, They shall plant vineyards and drink their wine…Nevermore to be uprooted From the soil I have given them." And to hear people suggest that the Jews in Israel are colonialists. How outrageous!

I remember reading my Great Uncle Harry's report on his visit to then Palestine in 1936, when the Jews were still in their early pioneering days of their life in Israel, taking a land largely barren and starting to bring to it a new revival. When I was there in 1963 and taken on a short tour by legendary opera singer Jan Peerce and his extraordinary wife Alice Peerce (another story and one I will treasure) in their limousine, they talked of how the land was coming to life with a new vibrancy as the Jewish people were returning to their homeland.

The pride of these early days need be remembered, not as a time of displacing Arab Palestinians, rather as a time that a dream was becoming a reality, the Jewish people were once again restoring their homeland. It's not been easy, these many thousands of years, as enemies have massed and been determined to remove the Jewish people from this Promised Land, sometimes succeeding, and fortunately in recent times with the strength and bravery of the Israeli people, being able to overcome every attempt to "throw the Jewish people into the Sea."

Wars were started by Arab countries surrounding Israel, and each time Israel defended itself. Each time may have meant the destruction of Israel, and the loss of a significant percentage of the Jewish people living in the world. Few countries stood with Israel, and yet they won each war. And when they won a war that others had started, the world made them withdraw from the land they had secured during the war.

President Obama in early 2010 told a group of Jewish leaders at the White House that they would have to engage in some serious "self-reflection." I wrote an article, "We Shall Bow Down to No One" soon thereafter, referring to my self-reflecting. Well, Mr. President, I continue to "self-reflect", for this is a most serious time for Israel and the Jewish people, with your Administration ending, and a new one about to be elected. And here's the issue I raise, "What does it mean in 2016 to be pro-Israel?"

Can someone be involved in supporting BDS, and still consider themselves pro-Israel? Can someone be a member of an organization such as J-Street or B'Tselem, and still be pro-Israel? Can someone call Israel an apartheid country, and still be pro-Israel? Can someone condemn Israel for their actions in the Gaza War in defending themselves as was done in the Goldwasser Report, and still be pro-Israel?

Can someone overlook the hundred thousand missiles facing Israel on all sides, not taking into account the security needs of Israel, and call for a peace treaty in which Israel would have borders that jeopardize the future security of the Nation?

Can someone overlook, and refuse to criticize the Arab Palestinians, both members of Hamas and now followers of Mahmoud Abbas, who celebrate, and even pay families for the deaths of Israelis at the hands of their own citizens by bombs and by knives? Can that person or organization consider themselves pro-Israel?

As an example, the advocacy organization J-STREET is not pro-Israel in my opinion. After years of having watched J-Street mimic and support President Obama and the White House, I received two J-Street e-mails just prior to the Party Conventions that really crossed the line. The first e-mail arrived, signed by Representatives Keith Ellison and Luis Gutierrez, both members of the Democratic Party Platform Committee with one appointed

Senator Bernie Sanders and the other by Secretary of State Hillary Clinton, and both known for their relative failure of support for Israel, if not outright opposition.

This first letter was about the Democratic Party Platform, and it started with their comment that they just returned from their trips to Israel and Palestine. It says that all in the Democratic Party agree to the core values, a two-state solution and an end to security concerns for Israel, and an end to the "unjust occupation" of Palestine by the Israelis. Simple to say it that way and it fails to clear any of the muddy water. Some may say, this does not sound bad at all.

A next e-mail arrived soon thereafter, and this one was from Alan Eisner, VP of Communications for J Street. He condemned Israel's continued building of settlements. Yes, he did comment that there was a horrific wave of recent terrorist attacks against Israelis. Then, he continued with, I suppose he would say in the words of J-Street, his Pro-Peace, Pro-Israel recommendations for the future. Here they are: (1) The United States should return to calling settlements "illegal"; (2)on future UN resolutions where settlements are condemned, the US should not use its veto; (3) that any Israeli extension of existing settlements should be seen as establishing a new settlement in violation of international agreements; (4)enforcement of customs regulations requiring products be labeled from territory over the Green Line (essentially a basis for BDS), and (5) report back to the President on tax deductibility of West Bank products.

Nobody will convince me that this letter from J-Street can be interpreted as Pro-Israel. It was potentially dangerous to Israel and was an ominous sign as we headed into the Democratic Convention where J Street fully intended to have a significant hand in the tone and words for the Party's position on Israel.

Fortunately, the Democratic Party Platform clearly recognized the bias, and did not reflect this full positioning in its Platform.

Where are our Major Jewish organizations and their leadership? This is anecdotal, and yes, it happened to me recently. I was stopped at a meeting of a major Jewish organization from saying my opinion, when I commented that I do not think J Street is supportive of Israel, that it is certainly not Pro-Israel as I define it. Yes, stopped, even though someone right before was able to comment on the positive support that J Street gives to Israel. And this was at a gathering to discuss the danger of the BDS Movement, and what we in the Jewish community can do to counter it. Start with our own, I say.

I have watched as major Jewish organizations have missions to Israel for governmental officials and leaders of business who ostensibly are to be given a most positive look at Israel, and yet will not include in their itineraries any stops or travels in Judea and Samaria. There is an exception. Yes, these leaders are taken over the Green Line to Ramallah to meet with the Palestinian leadership, and in one case that I heard about, an Orthodox Jew was asked to remove his yarmulke because the Palestinian Arabs objected to his wearing it there.

I watch as time and again there is no mention of our Jewish heritage and rights in Judea and Samaria. To think of our history in Shiloh, capital of King David's kingdom, and Hebron, where our ancestors lived and faced a pogrom by the Arabs in 1929, and the Biblical step-by-step recorded history on that land of Judea and Samaria that is never mentioned, except to say that Israel is occupiers there, and needs to give it up. The American Jewish community needs to voice the significance of Judea and Samaria to the future of Israel. And it needs to remember, that we liberated our land in the 1967 Six-Day War started by the Arab countries against Israel.

Both the government in Israel and a majority of the people in Israel now recognize Israel's need for remaining on a significant portion, if not the entirety of Judea and Samaria. I believe that Israel should declare sovereignty over this land, annex it in its entirety, and I have voiced that for years. Now more than ever, though, our organizations and leadership, with the threat of missiles potentially raining down on Israel, with the Hamas leadership bound to take over the future State of Palestine if it were ever formed on the West Bank, with the inherent threat voiced continually by the Palestinian Arabs that they want to take over the entirety of Israel, must redefine their Pro-Israel positions.

This should have been a golden period for Israel. Yet too many of our organizations, and their leadership, have stood quietly while this Obama Administration has, to be kind, been disrespectful to Israel and its leadership. In a Middle East that is embroiled in turmoil, death and destruction, Israel has been a shining light of democracy and peace. Realize in recent years that Israel has faced, and endured its own terrorism, which is hardly given attention, and faced, and won a serious war, in which the US government threatened to cut off supplies when they were needed, and even called for the stoppage of all flights to Ben Gurion Airport. It took an extraordinarily bold commitment of Mayor Michael Bloomberg to step on a plane and fly into Ben Gurion Airport, to break the embargo on flights.

New Pro-Israel leadership must now be noticed in America. The American leadership for standing with Israel includes a new group of actors, some around a long time and not noticed, and others newly formed who are not limited by their political correctness to the world at large but led on by their unwavering commitment to the State of Israel. And there are Israeli organizations, with American Friends counterparts, that are now outspoken about Judea and Samaria.

This new Pro-Israel leadership now recognizes that the future of Israel is not secure, and the two-state solution is not sacred. The leadership of the Palestinians has shown time and time again that their motive is not peace together with Israel, it is peace in place of Israel. They teach it in their schools where they train their children at the earliest age that it is good to fight Israel and the Jews. They show it when they pay the families of terrorists who stab or shoot and kill Israelis and celebrate often with parades for the martyrdom of these terrorists.

We must recognize the reality on the ground. We can never be cowards. The radical Islamists are at war, in a most serious way. Jews were expelled from practically all Arab Countries in the mid-20th Century after having civilizations there for hundreds and thousands of years. Today, Christians are being decimated in their remaining villages and towns in the Middle East by today's Islamic radicals, and their population is dwindling, and their long-standing civilizations are ending.

And we must stand with Israel during these days of turmoil, as it tries to preserve a Christian, Muslim and Jewish civilization in Judea and Samaria, and to preserve the historic Jewish attachment to the Temple Mount. The Arab Palestinians have pushed Christians out of Bethlehem, are mandating that all Jews must leave Judea and Samaria as part of any proposed peace agreement, and among an increasing radicalized minority of their population, remove all Jews from the entirety of Israel, or as they say, push the Jews into the Sea.

As the radical Islamist tyrants now press their beliefs into Europe and Northern Africa, we must stand our ground in the Land of Israel, for our entire civilization's future is at stake. Some may say that Mahmoud Abbas and the Arab Palestinians are moderates, and this cleansing will not happen. We watched Gaza as withdrew, and Hamas took over and turned it into a radical Islamic State with Sharia Law and no Jewish people, and we know that Hamas will take over Judea and Samaria if Israel should leave.

So, although I was so hopeful after the Oslo Agreement that we could have a two-state solution, with a demilitarized Palestinian State living prosperously together with a secure Jewish State as peaceful next-door neighbors, that time has passed. That's no longer the prospect for a Palestinian State, and no longer a possibility for the peaceful future of the region, although a recent creative, bold suggestion for an expanded Gaza with an artificially built island off its coast with an airport and seaport could well be a basis for a future Palestinian State.

I have always felt that our generation, born with the State of Israel, has a greater responsibility than many other generations to carry the torch, and to ensure that it stays lit for posterity. We have been through darkness, and this is the era of light for our people. Clearly, something beyond our day is being written, nearly like a Biblical new Chapter, with the story of our Jewish people's return to Israel. Yes, this is our moment.

Certainly, Israel is raising issues that we must face, and that cause many of us consternation. The religious governance in Israel may not be to our liking, as the orthodoxy controls the guidelines for religious observance in Israel, with little room for conservatism and reform views and practices. We are concerned about the treatment of the Arab population in Israel, as we are about the Palestinian Arab population in Judea and Samaria. And we may be concerned with some other practices of the Israeli government and Israeli people.

We do have a choice today, much larger in scope, one that we have not yet accommodated to. Perhaps our leadership is thinking too small. Whether out of illiteracy of our Jewish people's history, their own secular political correctness, their guidance by the power and significance of fundraising, or their relationships to those in power that they are trying to protect, the leadership is thinking only about today, and not yesterday and tomorrow. They take pride in their positioning, and I see hypocrisy in many of them.

There is not a realization that we were in exile from the Land of Israel for two thousand years. There is not a realization of the uniqueness, the extraordinary nature of our people maintaining our spirit and the determination of our cause for all those years. Over the years in exile, and in Diaspora, we made our way very successfully in lands throughout the globe, as we continue to today. And yet, the Binding spirit was a return to the land that God had given us, and had guided us to, our Land of Israel.

We have a transcendent responsibility, both to our ancestors and to our future generations, to remain on the land of Israel that we hold today, including Judea, Samaria, and the entirety of Jerusalem. The words written in the letters of J-Street are words of Jewish hypocrites who either out of their being human do not see things clearly at times, or, and this is darker, their words, knowingly, are expressed to be uncaring, perhaps truly harmful to the Jewish people and the State of Israel. In either case, we must take a long look, for if a person or organization by their comments or actions are not worthy of being considered Pro-Israel, in a real sense, we must take a strong stand to position them outside of our Jewish mainstream.

With the recent death of Elie Wiesel, and the attention during his life that he focused on the Holocaust, I must add one point that we should never forget. In his book, Mein Kampf, Hitler had his own understanding of the Jewish people. One of his tenets was that the Jews would never set up a state of their own, that they would always live off others. Clearly, Hitler was wrong! Our Jewish people have had a strength of character, and spirit, and soul that has led us once again, resulting in the return of an extraordinary people to its own land after 2,000 years in exile.

The Israeli people have built a magnificent state, Israel, a leader in democracy in the Middle East, a leader in technology, a strong military power, a dynamic, growing center for human development in culture, the arts, now reaching out to Africa and other regions throughout the world to pass on their skills for the betterment of other peoples. And we must stop our apologizing, our thinking small, and proudly declare the unification of our ancient kingdom, Judea and Samaria with our current State of Israel, One Israel, a miracle of our time.

There is no occupation, you hypocrites, there is only a continuum that has been created so our Prophet Amos can look down and know that his words still have meaning and reality today. An early reviewer of this article commented that it sounds like "unadulterated Zionist propaganda." Well, in response, I said thank you, that I proudly am 100% Pro-Israel, Pro-Peace, and thrilled to be an unadulterated Zionist in the Year 2016.

FIGHTING FOR OUR RENEWED JEWISH ETHOS

April 2002

As we watch the Israeli Defense Forces bravely fighting to secure the safety of a future Israel, we also have a fight that we must take on here in America, for it is an important fight for the future of our Jewish peoplehood. It is the fight for our Jewish literacy, the understanding of our Jewish history, vision and destiny. And we must do it now. And then we must use it to speak out more forcefully. And we must be reinvolved on a more grassroots level on the issues of importance to our community.

For today, too many of our Jewish community who don't know who we are, and what we have fought for these thousands of years. If we were truly literate, then our ability to answer so many of the unanswered questions now swirling about would be easy. I say to those who have been asking, "What can I do to help at a time like this?", commit yourself with the intensity of the Israeli soldiers to restoring the literacy we have lost of our great Jewish heritage. Only then can we become an effective fighting brigade for our Jewish people, through a way that we have been trained as a Jewish people, through our ideas and our thoughts.

Here's how I approached it. I asked myself, "Where can one begin?" At this time of year, with Passover recently over and the Counting of the Omer underway, and with the continuing tragic events in Israel, look at G-d's instructions to Moses as he led the Jewish people out of Egypt and through the Sinai, toward the Promised Land.

I turned to my Bible, presented to me by the Sisterhood of the Huntington Jewish Center for my Bar-Mitzvah in 1959. According to the Torah, we were given the land of Israel, by G-d, to keep the Commandments, "Observe therefore and do them; for this is your wisdom and your understanding in the sight of these people, that when they have all these statutes, they shall say, "Surely this great victim is a wise and understanding people (Deuteronomy 4.6)."

And we were given the warnings by G-d, in Deuteronomy8.11, "Beware lest thou forget the Lord thy G-d, in not keeping his Commandments, and his Ordinances and His Statutes, which I command thee this day,"; in Deuteronomy 8.17, lest "thou say in thy heart: "My power and might of my Land hath gotten me this Wealth."; and finally, in Deuteronomy 8.19, "And it shall be, if thou shalt forget the Lord thy G-d, and walk after other gods, and serve them and worship them, I forewarn you this day that you shall surely perish. "As the nations that the Lord maketh to perish before you, so shall ye perish, because ye would not harken to the Word of the Lord your G-d."

G-d promised our people the land of Israel. If we broke our commitments, and didn't follow the Commandments, it could be taken away for a period of time. Upon our learning anew, and respecting, and following the G-d's commandments, we would be returned to the Land of Israel.

Interestingly, in Numbers 33.55, G-d warns Moses that, "But if ye will not drive out the inhabitants of the land from before you, then shall those that remain of them be as thorns in your eyes, and as pricks in your sides, and they shall harass you in the land wherein ye dwell. And it shall come to pass, that as I thought to do unto them, so I will do unto you."

I couldn't help asking myself, and then others: Does G-d have a role in the events today in Israel? If so, what must we learn and what must we do to fulfill our commitments to G-d in order to make Israel the full and continued reality promised by the Bible and G-d? And what message is G-d giving us?

As an example, one of the people I asked the questions was Devorah Halberstam, director of government services of the new Brooklyn Jewish Children's Museum in Crown Heights (dedicated to the memory of her son Ari, who was killed in 1994 in a terrorist attack on the Brooklyn Bridge because he was a Jew). She told me that Rebbe Menachem Schneerson ten years ago said that there will come a time when Israel will offer to give all the land back, and the Arabs won't accept it. Rabbi Schneerson, she said, had the opinion based on the Torah, that Israel was endowed to us by G-d, and we should not give back the land.

So, we must study our modern-day history, and become better advocates for the State of Israel and for our people, to help shape our future. As I tried to answer the questions, I looked at Triumph of Survival by Beryl Wein, given to me years ago by Sy Siegel, and also, I looked at Jewish Literacy by Rabbi Joseph Telushkin, given to me by Michael Stoler (Siegel and Stoler are friends deeply involved in Jewish life and community). I also spent several hours reading the English version of The Book of Legends (Sefer Ha-Aggadah), an extraordinary compendium of our Jewish thinking and Rabbinic legend and lore compiled by Hayim Nachman Bialik in early 20thCentury Russia.

In the introduction to the Sefer Ha-Aggadah, David Stern

argued that restoration to a geographical homeland was not enough. The danger was that though we "might succeed in physically restoring the Jews to their homeland, the spiritual regeneration of the Jewish people, the restoration of the Jewish ethos, would be overlooked in the process." Bialik compiled the volume precisely because he found in our literature the knowledge of the "Nation of Israel, the secret of the Jewish genius, of the national ethos."

I read about Hatikvah, The Hope, the national anthem of Israel from a poem written by Hebrew poet Naftali Hertz Imber who died in 1909. We sing it all the time, or at least hum along, and it says in part: "Our Hope is Not Yet Lost/ the hope of two thousand years/ to be a free people in our own land/ the land of Zion and Jerusalem.

I thought about a young Israeli, then 28 years old, who commented to me a couple of years ago at The Salute to Israel Parade office, that he doesn't understand why American Jews would have such a parade. He was doing a documentary on the parade, so young Israelis would understand. When I told him we shared a 2,000-year period of praying for our return to Eretz Yisrael, and we shared a common interest in its future, he couldn't yet fathom the connection.

Lord Balfour, then Prime Minister of Great Britain, in 1917, gave a real nudge to the process of rebirth when he declared that he favored a national home for the Jewish people, and for that he became a hero of the Jewish people, and we should know that. The homeland was to be carved out of the Ottoman Empire, and the countries of Saudi Arabia, Jordan, and Syria were only then created in the 20thCentury, and Israel was to include all of the West Bank, including parts of all three of those countries.

Another piece of information we should know, the Jewish claim to the City of Hebron goes back to Biblical days. It is the burial ground for our matriarchs and patriarchs Abraham, Sarah, Isaac, Jacob, Rebecca, and Leah. Hebron is one of our holiest spots. Yet, we were forced to leave in 1929, when there was a pogrom of the Jews of Hebron. We resettled in 1931, were evacuated in 1936 under renewed anti-Jewish attacks, were not allowed to resettle there when it came into the hands of Jordan in the 1948 War of Independence, and only in 1967-8, were we able to visit, and once again live in one of our holiest places.

We must know our history, if we are to decide whether justice is served by our staying in Hebron forever. For me, the answer is yes. We should know why and be able to advocate for it. The Hebron Massacre symbolizes the Arab attempt to tell us that we should not be able to live in one of our holiest places, and the answer, for me is that is not acceptable. We cannot permit the Arab people, nor any people, from restricting us as they did from living in our historic city.

Lest we forget, and I remember because a group I then cochaired, called the Roundtable, made up of the Presidents of the New York Young Leadership organizations, held a rally in 1982, on the fifth anniversary of Israel's withdrawal from Sinai, and we called it "Israel's Sacrifice for Peace." The entire Sinai was returned to Egypt in the hope for peace, including full normalization of relationships with Egypt. And we gave up oil in Sinai. And we gave up resorts in Sinai. And we gave up training bases for the military and the Air Force. And we gave up Biblical land. That return mandated that we Jews could not live on that land, and the settlement of Yamit had to be pulled down, literally destroyed because we could not remain on what was then to become Egyptian land once again. All for the hope of peace.

In Jimmy Breslin's column in Newsday this past Friday, he quotes Irish American leader and lawyer Brian O'Dwyer (whose family has always stood together with the Jewish people and Israel), from a conversation he had with him on the way back from Washington, DC, relating a story from our trip to Israel with then Mayor David Dinkins in 1993. I say "we," because he mentions that "Howard Teich, Patricia Reberg, Suzan Johnson," and "Dr. Ruth" together with Father Mychal Judge all held hands, at Father Judge's request, and sang Silent Night in the Church of the Nativity in Bethlehem. And Brian O'Dwyer mentions, "It was quite a thing. If we went today, they would not let us in." Although when Israel controlled Bethlehem, it was open to everyone, Jews, Christians, and Moslems, today under Palestinian control, we cannot go there.

Don't forget with every right is a responsibility. We do have a responsibility to our neighbors, for in a modern world, which is part of being a light unto the nations. Together with anger, we must have empathy. And we must look at whether our values and ethos today as a people in Israel, and as a Jewish people throughout the world, the way we are living our lives and the way we are portraying them, is in keeping with our Promise. We must take responsibility for the bad and the good, and we must question our role, and G-d's role in the Jewish condition today.

This is a watershed time in Jewish history, a unique time for a generation born to the largest degree after the Holocaust and with the State of Israel. For our Jewish heritage, our destiny is in our hands. We are carrying the torch for our people. I was told that the late Israeli Prime Minister Yitzhak Rabin's daughter, last week on television, said that the Arabs must acknowledge that Israel is, and must be, a Jewish state. That is significant. Many of us take that for granted, and yet, that is not the position of some Jews in Israel, who see Israel as a democratic country to be proud of, but not necessarily a Jewish State. And that's what Israel must be accepted as by the Arabs and the world.

How we carry out G-d's will, and how we remain a light unto the world as a people who accepted the Torah, and who accepted the responsibility once again of Eretz Yisrael, and how we remain a modern people, that is not only an Israeli issue – it's an issue for all of us. And that responsibility that we have in Israel, and towards Israel, is also one that we have in regard to world Jewry. And we can make a difference.

We cannot make that difference, however, without knowing our history in Diaspora as well, and in America, we cannot do it without knowing of our great freedoms and achievements in America. New Yorkers have led the way in this past century, and it is time for a renewal of that dedication and energy, not just on a leadership level, but from the entire community. We've done a lot, and we haven't yet done enough. This is a time to remember our Jewish heritage and be proud of it. The months of April and May are the centerpiece of our Jewish Heritage NY2002 celebration. So study and go to one or more of the many events and activities that are taking place. Come out to show your support at the Salute to Israel Parade on May 5thand at rallies around town.

And most importantly, use the thoughts of this article to question your friends and others, study, and make demands on your Jewish leaders, and speak out for what you believe. In the Sefer Ha-Aggadah, Rabbi Yohanan is quoted as saying, "Why is Israel said to be like the olive? Because as the olive will not yield its oil unless it is crushed, so Israel does not return to the right way unless they are crushed by affliction." Let us use this most difficult period to find the right way, for we all must be fighters on the front lines, for ourselves and for our people, whether in Israel or in New York.

NO LONGER SILENT: NO RETREAT FROM GUSH KATIF

June 2005

April, 1982. We commemorated Israel's Sacrifice for Peace at Park East Synagogue in Manhattan. It was the completion of Israel's multi-year withdrawal from Sinai, giving back a land-mass larger than the entirety of today's Israel to bring peace and normalization.

I remember being in Yamit, a wonderful town built by Israelis in the Northern Sinai, with greenhouses and flowers, children and families, bringing life to the desert. That was before Jews were forced to leave Yamit by the Israeli government, seeing their homes torn down. The first land for peace deal brought desert back instead of maintaining life.

Many of the same Jewish families of Yamit moved from Sinai to the Northern Negev to live in Gush Katif in the early 1980's, continuing their dream of making the desert bloom, and creating a life on new land for themselves and future generations. And it was not only their dream, it was the dream of then Prime Minister Golda Meir, Yitzhak Rabin, and Ariel Sharon.

Today, Gush Katif thrives with nearly 10,000 residents in 21 communities. I just recently learned some other specific facts, important facts that I share with you. Exports from Gush Katif total $100,000,000 annually, producing 95% of Israel's bug-free lettuce and greens, 70% of its organic lettuce, 60% of its cherry tomatoes, as well as 60% of its geranium exports to Europe. Its community of Atzmona has Israel's largest flower and plant nursery, and the Katif barns with 800 cows are the second largest in Israel.

The point being this is no small settlement. This is a solid community with solid enterprises composing what we'd call a township or perhaps a county, with a full complement of activities and institutions. As an example, there are 40 kindergartens for the children, and 36 synagogues, with a membership of 450 in one alone. There are 50 stores and a community and cultural center, 3 beaches, and beautiful houses and gardens. All this would be erased for the Jewish people.

We, as Jews, are about life. Le Chaim. We best take a hard look at what we are being asked to accept in giving up on life in Gush Katif, and asking, no, forcing Jews to leave their land and their homes, their life. Jews forcing Jews to leave is a very dangerous precedent, and there's time yet to say, NO, and that's what I now say in this article, which reflects my thinking.

I am not a crazy activist. I am someone who has devoted a most significant part of thirty plus years to the Jewish community, taking leadership roles in many Jewish organizations. I know I cannot be silent now on an issue that is as important as any that I have weighed in on during these years. For I was essentially born with the State of Israel, and it is the responsibility of my generation to safeguard Israel for future generations. Although I may not live in Israel, I am equally committed to the future of Israel as those who do live in Israel.

We must never forget what Israel has already sacrificed for peace when we view this one-sided retreat from Gaza. It should not take place without a commensurate action of substance on the Palestinian side. And that is not happening. Terrorists are not laying down their arms. They are strengthening, emboldened by what they can only see as the weakness under pressure of the Israeli government. No one can convince me that Arabs seeing Jews being forced to leave their homes by the Israeli government can serve a future of peace.

Here's a basic premise for me that cannot and must not be broken. No Jew should be forced to leave any land. There is no excuse, nor any reason, for a Jew in the 21st Century not to be able to live in any land of choice. If Jews want to remain in Gaza, then clearly they should be able to. For a Jewish leader in Israel to force them to leave is really a mark on our Jewish people. And anyone who remains silent, and allows this to happen, is simply an accomplice in a future not of peace in Israel and in Diaspora, but of a Jewish world once again straining for survival.

Think of the future in what Israel is doing now, and the implications are grave for all of us. You set up a situation in which a precedent is established far beyond the borders of Israel. Removing Jews for safety in today's world is no longer security, it is preparation for self-imposed long-term suicide. There is a time to take a stand, and it is now. How many more places in this world that had Jewish civilizations for centuries and millennia should be cleansed of Jewish populations in our time.

Haven't we learned anything from our history? Are we so blind that we don't see or don't want to see that the enemies of Israel won't be satisfied except to have their return to the entirety of Israel, with the destruction of the Jewish State? I want to believe differently, and yet there is little evidence to give me optimism.

Today, there is so little talk of one, unified Jerusalem as the capital of Israel, and virtually no pressure on our United States government to move its embassy to Jerusalem. Only a few years ago, this was a priority and was an expectation. Just as a requirement only a few years ago was a demilitarized Palestinian entity, and today that no longer appears to be a requirement. Israel keeps giving, with little in return.

Well, it's time that there be a change, and we who have been silent speak out. Enough! Unless the surrounding Arab countries recognize Israel, and start the normalization of Israel, then Israel, with Judea and Samaria, Gaza and the Golan, and the entirety of Jerusalem should remain status quo as part of Israel. For Israel has made its great sacrifice for peace, with little resulting thankfulness from its neighboring countries and from the world.

We, as a Jewish people, were led into Israel in Biblical times, and our return to Israel was for secular reasons in protecting the future of the Jewish people, and for religious reasons as part of a continuing covenant with G-d. The surrounding Arab countries, and the world, in 1947, 1956, 1967, 1973, and until now, have done their utmost to limit the landmass of Israel, and to harm the Jewish people. We must recognize that fact, and stand our ground in Gaza, and not retreat from Gush Katif.

We as a Jewish people must not be divided, as we were 2,000 years ago, for we will lose Israel once again. We must be one, unified Jewish people, in Israel and in Diaspora, to tell the world that we are entitles to the land of our heritage. Where we have a thriving community of Jews, we must tell the world, we will no longer accept that we will be forced to move. And the issue of Gush Katif is on the front burner today.

It is ironic that in 1947, Egypt could make a land-grab of Gaza, and in fact Jordan, of the West Bank, without a whimper from the world, and yet today Israel is under the greatest pressure for remaining. We must know our history and believe that we will be protected from fighting for long-term justice in Israel. The world constantly must be reminded that we will neither be pushed around, nor be afraid. And that particularly pertains to leaving lands when the going gets tough. It deserves an outcry from all our Jewish people that the Israeli government is not standing up for our people now in Gaza.

The line in the sand must be drawn at Gush Katif.

"NOT NOW, NOT EVER"

October 2006

Israel is faced with among the most dangerous conditions I have seen in my lifetime. There are choices that need to be made today. Prime Minister Olmert has said, after the debacle of the unilateral retreat from Gaza, and the apparent retreat five years ago from Southern Lebanon without any guard against the strengthening of Hezbollah that directly led to the recent war with Israel's Northern neighbor, that his unilateral withdrawal from the West Bank is "on hold for now." I say to him that I am 100% opposed to giving up the land.

I remember when the concept of Land for Peace was born amid great hopes for Israel and its neighboring Arab states. I remember when the Jaffe Center reported out its study years ago among great criticism in the Jewish community, showing the need to give up the West Bank and Gaza, or face the loss of a democratic Israel through future demographic factors. I remember then Mayor of Jerusalem Olmert standing at City Hall in New York, boldly speaking out for the future of Jerusalem as an undivided city, the eternal capital of Israel and the Jewish people under Israeli sovereignty.

And what is the policy of the Olmert Government that is now

"on hold." The plan is to remove Jews living in Judea and Samaria from their homes, and to set new borders for Israel near the Green Line. Although this plan provides for keeping portions of the West Bank, 90 % of the land would be given back, including parts of Jerusalem.

After the recent war with Lebanon, and now recognizing the extraordinary danger of missile attacks on Israel, the land of Judea and Samaria is more important to Israel than ever. In negotiation after negotiation, that land was on the table. I say it should now be taken off, all of it. The Palestinians have shattered every attempt to create a peaceful resolution to their continuing war with Israel, and no longer should we be apologists for them.

If choices are to be made, then let's make them. The Olmert government's "Land for Surrender" policy does not work, so let's never consider it again. Then, let's declare "Land for Peace" as a policy discontinued, and dead. It does not, and will not work. This Oslo terminology should be dropped from our lexicon. No agreements have been kept by the Palestinians, and we really must see them as they are.

Hamas is the ruling party of the Palestinian people if we believe in their elections and democracy, and if they want to develop a state, they have the land to do it on the land in Gaza which they now control. I was opposed to the Sharon/Olmert Government's removal of the Jewish community of Gush Katif, and I am not surprised that the Palestinian people there have been more concerned with creating a terrorist stronghold to attack Israel than to foster a future of peace and success for their own people, notwithstanding the continuing Abbas charade.

As to the West Bank, the land of Judea and Samaria, it is clearly not occupied land. That land is clearly part of the ancient homeland of the Jewish people. It's time that we Jewish people take a renewed view of our vision and mission in being back in our ancestral homeland and recommit ourselves to the entirety of the traditional homeland of the Jewish people. We have it now for the first time in nearly 2,500 years, and we must not give it up. It is our history, and our ancestry. We should declare it as such, and unite it with present day Israel proper, and start building a strong future for those people living there, both Arab and Jew, as part of a new Israel.

Yes, it's true I don't live in Israel. I am not on the front line of today's battle. Some would say I have no right to speak out on Israel policy. I disagree. I am part of our heritage. And that means I have a responsibility for our generation, and the generations to come. That's the way we have always been as a people. We have always looked to the future, to redemption. The policy for Judea and Samaria is not a limited Israeli political issue, it is a moral and spiritual issue for the Jewish people in Israel and in Diaspora, and I have the obligation to speak out.

This is a time for a new policy of "Peace for Peace," with a blueprint in place for building a future in confidence for all the people in the entire land of Israel, and those others who want to cooperate with Israel. Let's truly be a light unto the world. Think about the dangerous future with a Palestinian State in Gaza and the West Bank, terrorist states on all sides with the unimpeded possibility of mortally wounding Israel and the Jewish people. Clearly, that would be the most likely scenario unless the policy changes I have suggested are implemented now. Future generations would be facing continued poverty and war, rather than peace and prosperity.

it would require a commitment to building and rebuilding the infrastructure of the Arab sections of the West Bank, which have been so significantly deteriorated under the leadership of Arafat and his successors. It would require a revitalization of the working relationship of Jews and Arabs, and the taking down of walls and barriers between the peoples. And it would require the enforcement of a lawful society in Judea and Samaria, where all people could live in security and peace, with a potentially prosperous future for all.

Is this unrealistic? I think not. Yes, the world would be initially aghast. But it would see peace and progress develop, and perhaps its eyes would reopen to a new possibility. I would rather see this future for Israel and the Jewish people, one that would give peace to the Jewish people, long-life to the Jewish State, and progress for its Arab citizens than a future of destruction that appears today.

So, Prime Minister Olmert, if it's unilateralism, then let it not be defeatism. Give up land in Judea and Samaria – "Not Now, Not Ever."

A DEFINING TIME FOR ISRAEL

June 2007

Some have compared the actions of Israel's leaders today to the appeasement of Britain's Chamberlain in dealing with Germany's Hitler just prior to World War II. I wasn't alive. I didn't directly experience it. I don't know.

Yet, with our 5,000-year history, and the survival of Israel potentially at stake, I couldn't be more disturbed by Israel's leadership today, for it affects all of us, Jews throughout the world, whether we live in Israel or not.

Israel deserted Gaza, leaving the Gush Katif towns and community to be taken over by Hamas, as a reality and as a legacy. Now, it is a terrorist state. Yet, the spirit of the pioneers of Gush Katif who were forced out by the Israeli government, and those who opposed the desertion, still exists. We must learn from their experience, and move forward with commitment and strength, for appeasement and weakness will not work.

Israel cannot risk another terrorist state on its borders. Fatah is not the answer, and cannot be trusted with Israel's destiny, no matter how much propping up there is... Israel must control its destiny. Israel must secure Judea, Samaria and Jerusalem forever. Israel must not, and cannot, risks its future and that of the Jewish people in diaspora. Yes, all of our futures.

Where are we 40 years after the victory of the 1967 War? Missing a certain optimism, and yet still in a position that we have liberated ancient Israel, with Judea, Samaria, and Jerusalem in Israel's control. It is time to take the next step in a world of danger and confusion, and that's to move to the next era, and declare the new, expanded borders of Israel.

It's time to turn to Israel's enemies, Hamas, Hezbollah, and others, and yes including Abbas, and say, you missed your chance. Now we're not any longer asking for your approval, we're declaring our G-d-given borders forever.

Here's my contention. After years of failed attempts to carve peace for the future in a formula of land for peace, wherein the West Bank would be a portion of a future Palestinian State, I say we can do more for the future of Israel, the future of the Jewish people, and I would contend, for the future of the Palestinian people, by annexing Judea, Samaria, and the entirety of Jerusalem now, and continue discussions as to the future of Gaza and the Golan.

Recently, in reading Martin Buber's, A Land of Two People, I specially noted his words written in 1939, "The correct response, pertaining to points of view on the Jewish-Arab question, "is a reaction to the moment not from the moment, but from the future. This is what we have missed every time. But we can still do it even today."

Martin Buber believed deeply that Jews and Arabs needed to live together if the future State of Israel was to succeed in a Jewish way, and I agree with him as we now see. The how is the difference.

Let's look from today and the future, looking back. How did we allow the word "occupation" and "occupiers" to be tied to Israel, stigmatizing the defense of Israel in 1967, its great victory against those countries that wanted to terminate its existence, and the rebirth of the Promised State of Israel in its full and its permanent borders? Why did we not annex the land or call it "liberated."

Why was the West Bank not "occupied land" when it was controlled by Jordan, when refugee camps existed from 1948-1967, and when those who lived in the land had no, or few rights under the Jordanian regime. The Arabs wrote the story, together with the rest of the international community.

The issue, however, is not outside of ourselves. Those who are part of 'the so-called peace camp or leftist camp" in Israel and in America, Jews not Arabs, who see no basis for Jewish control of the entirety of a united Jerusalem, Judea and Samaria (some are even embittered that we say Israel should be a Jewish State), must be questioned today as to their beliefs.

Articles written criticizing Israel for its human rights standards, when Arabs of Palestinian descent are let off the hook for being terrorists, destroying Israeli civilian mothers and children as well as their own people, whether for no reason or every reason, should now be held to account. They do not serve our people's long-term interests.

What would happen? A transformation of our people based on our history and heritage, our religion, and our move towards redemption. Once again, we must become one people, united for the future of Israel, and the Jewish people.

This reawakening, and responsibility, is not just in Israel, it is in World Jewry as well. We must stand up for the stronger Israel, dissipate world pressure on Israel to self-destruct, and educate the world of the great possibilities for the Israel promised to the Jewish people by G-d in the Torah.

We are the people who set a new standard in the world. We led, we did not retreat. We faced formidable opposition, and we overcame them.

I Have a Dream. It's our dream for a modern-day Israel. It's not necessarily the Palestinian dream. It's the Jewish dream. It's the dream of over 2,000 years. It's the dream of our heritage and our people. And we have it now, and all we have to do is keep it.

The miracle of Israel is here. We need to see it again. "Strength and courage," G-d said to our people when he told them to enter the Land of Israel. This was the entirety of the Promised Land, starting at the Jordan River.

Yes, the Jordan River, where Israel is today, yet we accept the terminology of "occupied land." It is not. It is land retaken, liberated, as part of what should be modern day Israel. Some would see this as part of the redemption. It is part of the Promised Land, of King David's Israel. Therefore, I ask again, how do we accept "occupied land"?

The 40th Anniversary of the Six-Day War has special significance, as one remembers the 40-year journey for Moses and the Jewish people as they wandered in the desert before being allowed to enter into the Promised land. Lessons had to be learned, and a new generation to be born and accept leadership.

Not much difference for us today. Forty years of attempts at peace, from land to peace, to creating a separate Palestinian State next to Israel. And what do we have? No peace, and an economically growing, spiritually uplifting, and a profoundly strong State of Israel. Perhaps we had to learn before we could enter in the 21st Century into Judea and Samaria, and the entirety of Jerusalem as our land.

"Here I am." Yes, we as Jews have found ourselves in the land of Israel, Judea and Samaria, the land that G-d gave to us as a people, taken away from us during our years of exile. Although we have secured the historical and Biblical land of Israel, our ancestral land of Judea and Samaria, and Jerusalem, are the international sources of pressure for creating peace by giving up the land.

In modern day terms, could it be any clearer that the only road to future peace is holding onto the land, redeeming the land as part of Eretz Yisrael, and creating on the land communities and opportunities that were prophesied? Don't we listen anymore? Don't we hear anymore? Don't we feel anymore?

Or perhaps the question is more aptly put, how many times are we told, how many times are we forewarned that we don't heed the message? Don't we have a body of ancient prophets who so aptly spelled out the warnings not only for their times, but for our age? How can we ignore them today?

I am saddened when I think that our people are so ready to give away our ancestral lands, our sacred lands that carry the history of our people, and that essentially carry the soul of our people. For whom are we, if not the descendants of that land that we are so intertwined with. Yes, who are we?

I have a dream that we will be restored to the entirety of the ancient homeland of the Jewish people, reunited in the land of King David. I dream of peace for our people, not a pretend peace advocated by false prophets who have their hope on words and dollars, rather a real peace that secures our Jewish people in land, in security, and in heart.

Yes, I have a Dream. I dream of Arabs and Jews living in peace, for we are both children of Abraham.

What do we need to change? We today have the land of Judea, Samaria, and Israel. We have reunited the Land of King David, as foretold in the Bible. And there are Arabs living on the land. With great wisdom and resources of Israel and the world community, we could give the Arabs in Judea, Samaria, and Jerusalem an opportunity far greater than their Palestinian brethren have in this land, and in other countries and territories. Otherwise, G-d gave us directions in the Bible, and even foretold what would happen if they insisted on being enemies. That would be their choice.

One hundred million Arabs have 98% of the land in the Middle East. It could all be questioned if one went back to the 1920's and 1940's, and yet we are referring to land claims of the Jewish people that go back thousands of years Our Jewish apologists and appeasers run to give back the land of our forefathers, our sacred land, and with no hope or reality of peace. They talk of it, rub shoulders with our enemies, blame Israel, and are the 21st Century's false prophets.

In an interesting recent private conversation with a so-called communal leader, I posed the question of annexing Judea and Samaria, recognizing the risk and reward, but holding a deep-felt belief that with G-d on our side we would achieve our goal, our destiny. He was Orthodox. I am not. He said to me he did not have that level of faith in G-d. That's the issue of our day.

Do we have faith in G-d, in our people, and in our destiny? And pragmatically, do we have trust, and believe in Israel and the IDF. Here I am. I do have that faith, that trust, and that belief. We can make it an extraordinary time for Israel, and World Jewry, as we commit as a Jewish people to ourselves and the world, that we can bring "peace to the Middle East, and if we follow from there, "peace on Earth, and goodwill to men." It is our challenge. It is our destiny.

Yes, it is a Defining Time for Israel and the Jewish People. We have liberated much of the Historic and Biblical Land of Israel. It is time to claim it finally and formally. It is ours.

THE NEW ISRAEL

November 2007

As we approach the year 2007, forty years will have passed since the liberation of Jerusalem, Judea, and Samaria by the Israel Defense Forces (IDF). That's the same number of years the Jewish people wandered in the desert after they left Egypt before they were allowed to enter into the Promised Land. And G-d in his words said to Moses (Deuteronomy 32:44) and Joshua (Joshua 1:6) as they looked beyond Jericho to the Land of Canaan, "Behold, this is the land that I swore unto your fathers, and this will be the land of your People."

This land was promised to the Jewish people, and although it remained under their control for many years, until it was liberated in the 1967 War, it had been under the occupation of many peoples, the last being the Jordanians. It is time that the historic recognition is effectuated, that this land be annexed as part of Israel in the earliest part of the Year 2007, and that Judea and Samaria become fully part of Israel for our generation and for the generations to follow.

In writing this article, I reached out to Mendy Halberstam, one of the brightest young Chassidic men I know, to discuss the Biblical and historic rights that the Jewish people had to the land known as the West Bank. We decided to collaborate on this article, providing a like-minded perspective of two very different members of our Jewish community from two separated generations, with a shared commitment to Israel and the Jewish people.

The Code of Jewish Law (OC § 329:6) specifically states that if a Jewish community, especially a border town, is attacked on the Sabbath, there is a clear obligation to react not only defensively, but also to take up arms and preempt any such attack. Though this would entail performance of work normally forbidden on the Sabbath, Jewish law properly sees such a potential threat to one community as a threat to the land rights and integrity of the entirety of Israel. When your neighbors attempt to undercut your rightful claim, you have an obligation to protect it. Until now, too many have accepted the Arab spin that Judea and Samaria is Palestinian land occupied by Israel. It's quite the opposite, for it is land of the Jewish people that was Arab occupied for many years until it was liberated in 1967.

It is not coincidental that we recently read in the Torah portion about G-d's promise of the land to Abraham. In the portion of Lech Lecha,(Genesis 15:18) G-d tells Abraham unequivocally "To your descendants I have given this land, from the river of Egypt... to the Euphrates river." Again in 17:8 G-d makes clear that "I will give to you and to your offspring...the whole of the land of Canaan, as an everlasting possession." The Bible could not be clearer of our territorial rights to every inch of the land of Israel.

We should be rightfully proud of the IDF's performance in the 1967 War, when Israel was attacked by its Arab neighbors. Israel did not invite that war, and yet they fought hard, and Israel recovered the land of our ancestors. Since that time, Israel has sacrificed land in the Sinai and the Golan Heights for peace treaties with Egypt and Jordan, and a limited truce with Syria. An elusive peace has remained a far distant possibility with the Palestinians and the remainder of the Arab countries as Israel has looked to trade land for peace.

Historically, peace had been refused to the Jewish people by the Arabs after the Balfour Declaration in 1923, which included Judea and Samaria as part of the new land for the Jewish people. Lost in 1947, the West Bank lands became part of Jordan, the declared Palestinian State under the agreements in 1948 when Israel was recognized at the United Nations.

Only after the 1967 War did the Palestinian people attempt to expand in defeat what they did not previously have, a State on the West Bank of the Jordan River. They nearly succeeded, with world opinion on their side, and the willingness of the Israeli governments to release most of the land to them to establish a Palestinian State. Now, it is even clearer that their intention was as they always portrayed it in their Arabic language and media, to terminate the existence of the State of Israel.

Consider that in the 1930's, the Arabs already aligned with the Nazis in Germany, directly pressured the British to not let Jewish refugees into Palestine. Why? Among other reasons, so they would maintain the demographic superiority in Palestine. They did not want an increased Jewish population, so the Jews were not allowed in, and many thousands, perhaps millions died in the Holocaust who should have been saved. The audacity of the Arabs to talk of greater numbers in Judea and Samaria today considering their actions, and their impact on the Holocaust, and what the numbers would have been today if they had not blocked an increased Jewish immigration at that time.

Some may say that we are rewriting history, and we say not. We are only correcting recent history which was being incorrectly written as we lived it. Historically, the Arabs have no claim to

Judea and Samaria. There was no such place as Arab Palestine on the lands of Judea and Samaria. Never. The current historical usurpation that so many have bought into is insulting, and derogatory to the reality of the Jewish people's claim, from Biblical times onward. When we left the land, it was only because we were forced to leave. The time we did not return, is when we could not.

Remember, since Talmudic times, our Jewish liturgy provides for the Jewish people to repeat three times per day in the prayers for our return to Zion, and the rebuilding of Jerusalem. Our forefathers and mothers, from Abraham to Rebecca, from Jacob to Deborah, from King David to Ezekiel, all have their deepest roots in Judea and Samaria. Whether it be in Hebron, or Jericho, or Bethlehem, we have our most sacred land, which our ancestors fought for and gave up their lives for. Land which we committed to G-d that we would not walk away from. Land in which are the bones of Jacob and Joseph, brought back from Egypt to be buried in our ancestral land. Land that was the original Land of Milk and Honey.

It is interesting that in his very first commentary on the Bible, the greatest Biblical commentator in our history, Rashi (1040-1105) informs us of the very events that would occur some one thousand year later. Rashi asks, "What is the reason the Bible began with Genesis? So that if the nations of the world say to Israel 'You are bandits, for you conquered the lands of the seven nations', Israel will say to them: The whole earth belongs to G-d, He created it and He gave it to the one found proper in His eyes. By His wish He gave it to them and by His wish He took it from them and gave it to us."

We must realize that there is a message, a reason we could not give this land away in negotiations during the past twenty years, when Arafat refused every possible offer. Today, there are no possible discussions for peace in Judea and Samaria other than annexation, when it is clearly apparent after the retreat in Gaza, that we would only face a fully armed territory with missiles ready to attack Israel proper from the East if Israel were to give up this land. Jordan is a good neighbor, and that's who the future neighbor should be.

Now, for those who are asking the questions of what faces the Jewish nature of Israel if there were to be annexation, and what would happen to those Arab Palestinians who are living on the land in cities like Jenin, Ramallah, Hebron, and other places throughout Judea and Samaria. This must be studied, and alternatives found. Here are some initial thoughts for consideration.

Since we talk only of the annexation of Judea and Samaria there would still be a Jewish majority in Israel, considering that the overwhelming majority of Palestinians live in Gaza. The Arab Palestinians from the newly annexed territory would have every right to live as citizens of Israel if they so choose, as they do today in Israel proper, and as they had been when they were living under Jordanian rule.

In fact, Israel would have to ensure the social welfare of the new Arab community in Israel. That would include living standards, education, safety, healthcare, and general quality of life. Enmity would have to be replaced by harmony on both sides. The world community would need to be supportive. In Deuteronomy, it is clear that the Jewish people have a responsibility to the treatment of our neighbors, even as we take over land that they may inhabit so long as they are not adversarial to us.

In that way, although the Palestinian Arabs would have choice, they would also have the responsibilities of citizenship. That involves being supportive of the State of Israel, dropping every intention to destroy its existence, giving up all their weapons intentioned for the destruction of Israel, and working hard to make Israel flourish. In this process of developing their citizenship which would entail respect for the rules and laws of Israel, we believe it would develop a more secure environment for all people living there. If any Palestinian would find it too hard to come to terms with the fact that Israel has and always will belong to the Jewish people, we revert to the concept of choice. Just as they would have the freedom to stay, they would have the freedom to leave.

Our priority, however, must always be the restoring and sustaining the entire state of Israel, our G-d-given right, our inheritance, our home, and that includes extending Israel to the Jordan River in the Year 2007.

WE MUST DRIVE OUR OWN DESTINY

February 2009

There is a bottom line for now. Peace negotiations for a two-state solution have been nearly disastrous and have led down a path that has not brought peace closer. Although those who push for that as the solution for peace are well-meaning, it will not work now, and it's time for American Jewish leaders to take their heads out of the sand, and forcefully and loudly support a strong and effective future for Israel on its own terms.

The Israeli population spoke in the last election, voicing the opinion that a two-state solution is off the table for now. They gave the message that continuing policy initiatives of the past are not the way to go.

Oslo has proven to be a false start. Retreating from Southern Lebanon only set up a new front for anti-Israel terrorists. The withdrawal from Gush Katif created a strongly militant terrorist state in Gaza that refuses to ever recognize Israel, and in fact calls for its destruction. And let's not forget earlier withdrawals from the entirety of the Sinai and parts of the Golan that Israel sacrificed in the name of peace. Israel has given back more territory than the size of its entire country today for the possibility of peace.

In return, Israel has faced intifadas in its own country, wars in Lebanon and then in Gaza, building of a wall to thwart suicide killings in Israel by separating Israel proper from its homeland in Judea and Samaria, attacks on Jewish citizens in Judea and Samaria, and an atmosphere threatened by a new Iranian power.

Additionally, there is an increase in anti-Semitic incidents in the world, directly related to Israel and the Islamic fundamental terrorists. Although money continues to flow at increasing rates into Palestinian territory, the people living there seem to be increasingly militant without increasing standards, economic development or a solid foundation for growth or peace.

Let's get it straight. After 61 years as a State, Israel is facing the threat of extinction by 100 million Arabs who surround it, from the Palestinians on its borders to the Iranians thousands of miles away. The Arabs remain unwilling to let Israelis live in peace. Going back to 1947 and before, the Arabs used the term Palestinian to gain additional land from the Jewish people and succeeded then. We cannot let that happen again.

The Land of Israel today is on the historic land of the Jewish people dating back to Moses and before. That land included Judea and Samaria as well as Jerusalem and Gaza, and in fact, a significant part of Lebanon and Syria. Through wars and extermination, the land of the Jewish people was reduced in size by foreign occupants until the Land of Israel was re-established and recognized by the world community.

Multiple wars later, the Jewish people continue to fight for their right to have a homeland. The Arabs refuse to recognize this reality, and continue to use force, and now diplomacy, world opinion, and terrorism, to destroy Israel. That's the facts on the ground. The Arab world's attempts to thwart peace with the mission of ridding the Middle East of a Jewish civilization must be seen for what it is, and brought to an end.

And there must be no acceptance of lands where Jews are forbidden to live. How outrageous to think that a peace agreement that is being proposed and discussed is set on the foundation of all-Arab territory, where Jews would not be able to live, whether it be Gaza, or Judea and Samaria, or even as it was with Yamit in the Sinai.

So, yes, it is time for a change. Certain principles guide my view.

First, Israel should never again retreat from land it possesses. It has no obligation to do it. Of paramount importance, we cannot accept the principle that Jews should not be allowed to live any place in this world that they choose to live. I would have hoped that we would learn that we can never accept again the word "judenrein" when it applies to our Jewish community.

The second principle is that Israel cannot turn our enemies into friends through retreat, only through strength. That was one of the earliest teachings of the great Founders of Israel, Ben Gurion among others, and the lesson remains the same today. The Palestinians and other Arabs, and the Iranians' words of destruction of the State of Israel must be taken seriously.

The third principle is that we must be proud of our Jewish heritage, and our return to Israel (yes, perhaps the term Greater Israel for purposes of understanding my intent). The original vision of Israel in the Bible encompassed the land west of the Jordan River, including our previous kingdoms of Judea and Samaria, the entirety of Jerusalem, and the land of Gaza. Israel has every right to exist in that land forever, and its claim is not secondary to that of the Palestinian Arabs. I reject the concept and the terminology that the lands are occupied territories.

The fourth principle is the clearest for me. Israel can never enter into a peace agreement unless it can be convinced that it will both offer a real long-term peace and will negate the probability of enhancing the strength of Israel's enemies.

We must remember certain facts. With the great wealth of

the Arabs, and their vast resources of land, the Palestinian people could be guaranteed by their brethren Arabs an incredible future on their land if they so choose. Jordan was to be the Palestinian State, and they threw many of their Palestinian people out of their country. Continuing the United Nations refugee camps has only continued the hardships of many of the Palestinian people. It is clear that the plight of the Palestinian people will not be resolved necessarily by an independent Palestinian State.

Although I opposed the withdrawal from Gush Katif, it was done, and Gaza was put into a position for the Palestinians to demonstrate that they could establish a positive society on their own land. They did not, and the fact is that Hamas set out in Gaza under Iranian guidance to disrupt, if not destroy Israel. That cannot, must not, and will not be.

Until the day that the Arab Palestinians accept Israel's right to be a Jewish State, their leadership credentials remain clouded. There can be no peace with them, and no one should be pushing Israel into a peace that is no peace at all.

It is time that American Jewry recognizes realities on the ground and stands firmly with Israel on them. We must be steadfast in our paramount interest that Israel's right to determine its own future is non-negotiable.

Soloveitchik said regarding the Holocaust, as I learned from the Simon Wiesenthal Center's new Moriah film, *Against the Tide*, "we must drive our own destiny, and transform fate into destiny during our life." This must be the commitment of world Jewry today.

We may not live in Israel, and yet living in America it is clear we can do something they cannot do alone. We can shout out with a clarion call, and proudly that Israel exists, and is entitled to a secure future just like every country on Earth. We must convince the World. *Am Yisrael Chai!*

WE SHALL BOW DOWN TO NO ONE: AMERICA'S JEWISH LEADERS MUST BE OUTSPOKEN IN SUPPORT OF ISRAEL

April 2010

Months ago, President Obama told a group of 15 Jewish leaders invited by him to the White House that Israel would need to engage in some "serious self-reflection." I interpreted his words to mean that I, as well, should self-reflect on my position. I voted for him, and I wanted to follow his lead. I did and I have, and here's what I have to say.

Our responsibility now as Jews in America is to be outspoken in our support of Israel, particularly when we see an apparent shift in policy by our president, which is neither in America's nor Israel's interest. And particularly when it may have a negative backlash against Jews in many parts of the world.

Silence has never served us well. Appeasement has never

served us well. The fate of Israel may be in our hands, and too many of our leaders have been quiet or conciliatory. This is unacceptable. We must believe in ourselves, and count on ourselves. When I self-reflected, a number of thoughts came to mind that are worth retelling for I considered several perspectives and came to very decisive views which I now share with you.

I am a Jewish American of the generation of the State of Israel. Unlike my ancestors, who could only pray for the return to Israel and Jerusalem for nearly 2,000 years, my responsibility has been to do what I can to ensure that we maintain the continued existence of Israel, with Jerusalem as its eternal, undivided capital.

During Pesach, we retold the story of the Exodus from Egypt as if it happened today, and we renewed and celebrated our freedom obtained after many years of slavery. And in how many other societies, and how many other eras could we retell how our people were kept in perceived, or actual slavery and loss of freedom? And as Moses did in Egypt, we saw the importance of standing up for our people.

If there is one lesson we learn from Pesach, it is that you can never take your freedom for granted and you must always fight for freedom. That includes the right to be in the land of your choosing, as a Jew. We have a long way to go for that freedom. How many countries today have a Jewish community in exile because they were forced out of their homes and communities? And it's not just our past. During my lifetime, whether it was in Arab countries or other countries where great Jewish civilizations have ended, the exile continues.

In Israel, I saw it in Yamit in the Sinai nearly 30 years ago when Jews were removed as part of an agreement that returned Sinai to Egypt, and again in Gush Katif in Gaza just a few years ago. Both sacrificed our people's growing, wonderful communities in the hopes of peace. Yes, Jews were forced out of their homes and made to leave their property, uprooted from their lives in an attempt to secure peace with their neighbors. So, please, don't tell us that Israel has not committed itself to peace.

Today, the Arabs continue the fight to take Israel away from us. I see the world telling us that we cannot live and grow in Judea and Samaria, and now in Jerusalem, lands that are part of our destiny going back thousands of years and, more recently, were given to the Jewish people in the Balfour Declaration, lands that were fought for against an enemy that attacked Israel on numerous occasions, attempting to annihilate her so she would no longer exist.

How outrageous to be told that Jews must not build for it is an obstacle to peace, on what amounts to a few percent of the land of Judea and Samaria and, just recently, in Jerusalem. This is not the land of the so-called Palestinians; it is the land of my Jewish people. And I see communities of thousands emerge out of barren land, with universities not only for Jews, but also for Palestinians, restoration of biblical centers and religious sites, and the potential for a growing civilization in our land to carry out the continuing legacy of my people.

And I cannot and will not stand by silently as I see calls that limit where Jews can live or how they can expand their civilization on their rightful, and historic, land. And I cannot remain silent when anyone restricts our human right to have land of our choosing, most recently when there is an uproar over plans for Israel to expand building for its citizens in Jerusalem.

So, yes, I will continue to self-reflect, as requested. I will speak out and urge others who I believe have been a silent mainstream of the Jewish community in America and in Israel. I will tell them that not only are so-called settlements not an obstacle for peace, they are a mainstay of a future peace and our Jewish civilization.

I will stand with those pioneers and heroes who are carrying out for so many of us the front-line commitment to our history's compelling destiny, not as enemies of others, but as developers of a civilization to create a longtime future for us, and for our neighbors. And I would recommend to everyone that if you cannot go there, go on the Internet and learn first-hand about them, and be in communication with them, and join in unity with them.

Remember, we don't have to be shy about our own people who are standing up for us, and not turning our land over to those who only want the termination of our people. We must be supportive and outspoken in favor of the present government of Israel, which faces increasing pressures and tough choices. And we must let the American leadership know that we stand 100 percent with Israel and will not let them denigrate Israel anymore.

The real story of Judea and Samaria for our Jewish community is similar to how I recently heard Buzz Aldrin, the first man to step on the moon, describe the importance of our space exploration — from pioneers to settlers to developers of new civilizations — with pride in the process.

We must look at Judea and Samaria with the same pride, to achieve our Jewish dream of returning to our Jewish, biblical, and historic roots. A new wave of our Jewish community returned in the late 19th to early 20th century as pioneers, faced obstacles, and brought more settlers to create out of nothing what are today modern Jewish communities and cities We've brought agriculture, industry, life and developed a civilization, been a light, with a great future ahead. And it doesn't have to be about displacement, it could be about living side-by-side in a Jewish State of Israel with prosperity and peace. That's a choice that the Arabs and Palestinians have to make.

In that regard, I am proud and supportive of Israel's recent actions.

A tree planting is an extraordinarily important symbol, for it represents the planting of roots for future generations of Jewish children. Prime Minister Benjamin Netanyahu planted trees over the Green Line for Tu B'Shevat, in the communities of Ariel and Ma'ale Adumim, thereby erasing a fabricated line in order to unify these communities into a future Israel. Realize that Ariel is a city of 20,000 residents and 10,000 university students; Ma'ale Adumim is a city of 40,000 people.

It's a sign of renewed vigor for a society that has been held to a higher standard and, I might add, one it has maintained against all odds. Surrounded by 100 million Arabs, most of whom still call for her to be driven into the sea, Israel has developed as a leading light in the world, and a country deserving of praise.

Shaul Goldstein, chairman of the Gush Etzion Regional Council, had it right when he said that the tree planting represented "a clear statement to the world that we are going to stay there forever."

I commend Prime Minister Netanyahu and the Cabinet for approving a National Heritage Plan to connect Israelis and others to their national, cultural and historic history. The plan includes 150 sites in Israel, including two very significant sites — the Cave of the Patriarchs in Hebron and Rachel's Tomb in Bethlehem. Yes, there has been criticism for including the two sites over the Green Line, and I say it's one more example where they are saying to us, "No, you cannot maintain your holy sites," just as they have said to us, "No, you cannot live there." I reject both those premises.

Groups such as J-Street try to criticize Israel at every turn, and try to equate the actions of Israel with those of Hamas and Hezbollah. While they may be a peace group, they are not a pro Israel organization, as we would term it.

Why even mention them? President Obama gave them a seat

at the table, but they're a false group. Public officials are using them as a charade for casting votes and voicing opinions, whether it's on the Goldstone decision or so many others that are antithetical Israel's interests. Realize that the Israeli government does not recognize them as a legitimate pro-Israel group. We must remain outspoken about their disruptiveness and divisiveness.

It's time for J-Streeters to see what we all see. Israel sent one of the first contingents of medical aid to Haiti and was a model of one country helping its neighbors in need. Israel's economy is a shining light in the world and its cultural institutions far outstrip any country comparable in size. Israel has made a difference in hi-tech, in science and in medicine. It has literally created a dynamic country out of a desert. And there is so much more.

Yes, Israel is endangered by enemies. And it has faced down those enemies who still continue to fire missiles into Israel, who hide behind their civilians when they fight and who feed future generation of Arab children with messages of hate in their classroom books.

Does Israel have more to do, and can it do better? Sure, that's true of every person and every country. We must stand up for the entirety of Israel. And all of our leadership, and our major organizations must speak out now, for the good of Israel, for the good of America and, candidly, for the good of the world.

I reject silence in the face of recent verbal attacks on Israel. I will continue to self-reflect, Mr. President, and with it I will become even more certain of the leadership role that I, and others like myself, must play in the Jewish community. We stand up proudly for what we believe and for our commitment to the 5,000-year heritage of our people. We shall bow down to no one.

TIME FOR ANNEXATION: NO EXTENSION OF SETTLEMENT MORATORIUM

August 2010

President Obama opens the gathering in Washington, DC last week with the words, "This moment of opportunity may not soon come again. They cannot afford to let it slip away." I agree, and yet, I am looking at the prospects differently than he is. This is not the Year 2000, and much has changed.

We have awaited this opportunity for 2,000 years, to have Judea and Samaria and the entirety of Jerusalem as part of modern-day Israel. Yes, now is that opportunity to guarantee it, and we must not lose that chance.

We need Judea and Samaria for Israel's security, as without it and the protection of the Jordan Valley, Jerusalem could be attacked within two minutes, Ben Gurion Airport would be impossible to defend, and most rockets would be able to strike the major Israel population centers with extraordinary destructive capability within minutes. Yes, now is that opportunity to broaden the safety zone, and we must not lose that chance.

We have 500,000 vibrant Jewish citizens of Israel in Judea and Samaria, and the eastern part of Jerusalem, and we must never again destroy our communities as was done in Gush Katif. and Yamit. We should have been asking, and demanding answers to why Jews would not be allowed to live in a Palestinian State, and demanding of the world to explain their acceptance of this premise. Yes, we must not lose the chance of having Jews living in our ancient homeland, promised by G-d.

And, we have the potential to work with the Palestinians who would remain on the land to continue to increase their individual standard of living, and secure their freedom of worship, and not risk losing that to Iranian-backed Hamas, and now is the opportunity to guarantee it, and we must not lose that chance.

There is a time for every deal to close, and the Palestinian Arabs may have missed their best opportunity in Judea and Samaria. Right now there are negotiations underway, and yet there are murmurings that Abbas will insist on an extension of the moratorium on Jewish building in Judea and Samaria. My answer to Abbas would be brief and simple, "We are building our future homes, and it's time for Israel to annex the land of Judea and Samaria." September 26th will be the day that Israel takes its rightful ownership of its Biblical lands. Now, let's talk peace."

For years Israel has offered incredible opportunities for peace to the Palestinian Arabs, and they have rejected all of it including offers to return nearly 100% of the land, with land-swaps. I say that the same opportunity should be taken off the table, and Israel must move on to develop the land, and secure its future.

Yes, secure its future. Most recent studies conclude that Israel can never give up the Jordan Valley, with today's threat of modern technology both in missiles and in cyber technology. The Palestinians failed to cut a deal before the Israelis faced a strengthened Hezbollah to the North in Lebanon, the increasing control of Syria by Iran, the radicalization of the Palestinians in Gaza, and most importantly the failure of Abbas to build a credible infrastructure for peace, and for a Palestinian State that would survive.

Abbas could not hold on to Gaza when he had the opportunity, and he has failed miserably notwithstanding enormous support from Israel, and worldwide aid, to show that he either wants to, or could successfully build a Palestinian State that would give Israel any sense of long-term security.

Just this past week, in keeping with longstanding Palestinian tradition, four vital, contributing, and essential Israeli citizens, one a pregnant woman, were brutally and calculatingly murdered in terrorist killings in Judea and Samaria. Of course, it is passed off as Hamas wanting to fracture the peace talks, and Abbas is let off the hook in the hope of continuing with the negotiations. I say it was Abbas' obligation to protect these people, and he either couldn't, or he was complicit in the killings. Either way, he has shown no ability to control security on these lands and protect human lives.

So, I say you had your chance, Mr. Abbas, as did your predecessor Yasser Arafat, and you failed your people, and Israel need not stop building, nor wait any longer to annex its Biblical land as a part of modern Israel. And your people have a choice, as Arabs have done in Israel since its birth, to have better lives than they have now, and become citizens of Israel. They will have to end their dream of destroying Israel, including changing school textbooks to change hate to support.

The land of Judea and Samaria was lost by the Arabs to Israel in the 1967 War, started by Arabs to destroy Israel. It didn't work out that way, and Jordan walked out of the land, for which they had only two countries recognize their control during their years of occupation. Yes, that's all. And the Palestinians never had a claim to the land. It was never Occupied Territory. UN Resolution 242 did not require Israel to return the land, and certainly the Resolution never had in mind using this same land to establish a Palestinian State.

So, I say we must fight for peace now, and we should be sitting with Abbas, but I say the parameters for negotiation must be changed. The possibility for a Palestinian State can still be discussed, and it should be limited to the land today called Gaza, which is today controlled by the terrorist organization Hamas.

And it's been threat after threat from Abbas and his Arab friends. And step by step, with the support of other Arab countries, and their people throughout the world, they have done their best to threaten and isolate Israel. Well, if they're following Allah, as they say, I have a G-d to lead me on, and to lead my people, and the Word was given millennia ago, "This is the Land that I Have Given to You."

So, with joy, and enthusiasm, I would support Israel's annexation of Judea and Samaria, and the incorporation of the entirety of Jerusalem, as part of Israel, and commit to being on the frontlines, as a United States citizen, to call on the President of the United States, Barak Obama, and the United States Congress, to recognize the annexation. This would be in the long-term best interests of Israel, of the United States, and of the great majority of the Palestinians.

THE VERY EXISTENCE OF ISRAEL IS AT STAKE: A CALL TO THE AMERICAN JEWISH COMMUNITY TO STAND UP IN HER DEFENSE

March 2011

You just want to start shouting at our Jewish people. It's time to come together and bring the world back to being our supporters. The Palestinian terrorist massacre at Itamar of a young, beautiful Israeli family must be the tipping point. Israel was once again restored to the land from the Mediterranean to the Jordan River in 1967 and we must never leave it.

Does the slaying in Judea and Samaria of an entire family, including three young children, by Palestinian terrorists finally bring some of our doubters back to reality? Whether it does or not, the Abbas charade must be seen for what it is a continuation of the Arafat effort to give a peaceful public face to a single-minded effort to destroy Israel. It is reported that the Aksa Martyrs Brigade, the military wing of Fatah, took credit for these murders. Just let that sink in.

Can we ever accept allowing our people to be murdered again in cold blood because they are Jews? Can we ever accept again that the answer to the Jewish problem is to cleanse the land of Jews? Can we ever have peace with a people who by their very acts demonstrate their intent to never accept, and their hope to destroy the State of Israel? And then, the even more difficult question, can we ever excuse our fellow Jews in this country who don't speak out at a time of crisis for Israel, or worse, try to appease those who directly support those who have every intention by their acts, to harm Israel and Israelis?

My answer is no, no, no, and No. In a clarion call, I appeal to the people of the world round to stand with the Jewish people once again, as they did in 1948. Agree that you will listen with an open mind, and then be supportive of working towards a time of peace with Judea, Samaria and the entirety of Jerusalem remaining part of the State of Israel. Yes, all Palestinians on the land would have fair and equal treatment and opportunity living in a future Israel, as Arab Israelis living in Israel today.

How many attempts for peace have been made in vain with the Palestinians, for the Palestinians are not interested in creating a State. They control Gaza, and they haven't moved towards a State. They were given back Southern Lebanon, and they turned it into an armed encampment, and the world has stood by and let it happen. The Palestinians have left their brothers and sisters in refugee camps when they could have easily moved them out into better conditions. And in the Sinai, they recently have cut off supplies of natural gas to Israel, and continually make efforts to sneak Iranian arms into Gaza to use against Israel.

So, I say it's time to put forward some Guidelines in America for the Future.

First, we must have zero tolerance for groups that support, or give aid and comfort to groups that conduct information warfare to delegitimize Israel or conduct economic warfare either through the Boycott Divestment and Sanctions (BDS) or other campaigns to directly harm Israel.

Second, all Jewish organizational missions to Israel must include in their itinerary visits to communities in Judea and Samaria, though over the so-called Green Line, as our people living in those communities, such as Itamar, are true heroes for a Jewish future in Israel, and we must show them our support, and ensure their safety and protection.

Third, we must demand of those people who consider themselves leaders of our American Jewish community that they speak out for the human rights of our fellow Jews living in Judea and Samaria. I particularly call on those who are involved in bridge-building relations with the Arab and Islamic communities in America, that they break those ties unless there is a willingness to have their Muslim partners speak out against the continued fostering of hatred against the Israelis by the Palestinians through their textbooks, their naming of street squares honoring terrorists, and their murders of innocent Jewish citizens of Israel and beyond, as in Itamar.

Fourth, now more than ever, we must show our support of Israel by personally visiting Israel including Judea and Samaria, buying Israeli products, particularly those made or produced in Judea and Samaria, and by speaking out forcefully when Israel is wronged.

There are people in our community who are often marginalized, now taking the leadership on these issues in a vacuum of leadership, and their stands are important. Pay attention to them, for they mean well, and their meaning is clear. Show up at their rallies and support their Internet outreach.

The new Jewish future requires increased literacy about who we are, and about the land of Israel. We need to develop more passion for our commitment to our people, and then increase our messages and actions of "compassionate righteousness" and "moral justice," our heritage from Sinai as written in the Torah. We must bring our stories of values, of service, and of moral clarity to the world.

We must present the case that Israel is our sacred homeland that we have liberated, and that we are committed to keeping every inch of. We must make the case once again how we have protected all religious sites in Israel, whether Christian, Jewish or Muslim. We must tell the extraordinary story of Israel, creating a vibrant democracy, and an economic miracle out of a barren land. And we must show an Israel that was first in Haiti and Japan with medical care in their times of need.

We must not hesitate to speak out about the threat we face, particularly from the Arab and Muslim community surrounding Israel and beyond. We can work towards peaceful relations, and never submerge our needs. In Israel, it's front-line on all sides. Keeping the Jordan Valley isn't just about the land, it's about security, and it's about Israel's very survival. If you haven't looked at a map recently, I suggest you do it.

The challenge is here and now. The very existence of Israel is at stake. Don't be afraid of jeopardizing your social status by standing up for what is right. Social acceptance doesn't require silence. Political correctness has no role. It is our generation's time to carry the torch of our people. Just What Don't You Get!!

WAKE-UP CALL: THE U.S. JEWISH COMMUNITY NEEDS COURAGEOUS LEADERSHIP

October 2012

The Arab Spring has turned into the Arab Winter, as we increasingly hear Israel is in a much more dangerous neighborhood as thousands of rockets are pointed toward the Jewish state by Hezbollah in Lebanon, Hamas in Gaza, from Iran's territory and potentially from the sea. Egypt and Syria are now unknowns.

The Obama administration is not Israel's best friend. We just cannot accept the president's statement that he "has Israel's back." It just does not ring true.

Prime Minister Bibi Netanyahu calls for Americans to take a stand on Israel's behalf against Iran. But America's and Israel's interests are different, or at least their timing may be different. America, based on its own interests, does not have to act now. Israel, though, may well have to make a move now against Iran's nuclear facilities to thwart the existential threat of the destruction of Israel as we know it, and the loss of a significant part of our Jewish people.

And yet there is silence from our Jewish establishment leadership in America. They are either close to Obama and don't want to offend him or compromise their relationship with him, or they face, as leaders, the limitation of consensus, meaning they cannot speak out if their organization does not have consensus, which many of our organizations require. Or, and this is important, their organizations do not support the Israeli government's positions.

So, we have silence at a time when we need to speak out.

It is incredible that for so many years the American Jewish left insisted we follow the policy of the Israeli prime minister when many courageous leaders of the Jewish right spoke out, giving early warning to policies that were not in Israel's interest in the long term. It was said that Israel belongs to the Israelis, and we in the American Jewish community must follow their lead if we are to be supportive. Today, when support is needed, they turn their backs, remain silent or oppose the positions of Israel.

The current dilemma is largely unprecedented, and the predominant issue for me is, what do we do about it? With Election Day upon us, it's an important question to ask in America. As American Jews, Israel is a factor in our vote, for some the deciding factor and for others one of many factors. Incredibly, when some members of our Jewish community consider the Israel factor, if a candidate or elected official is too pro-Israel, that's sufficient reason to vote against the candidate. Point being, consensus is not there, and thus we have silence and no leadership on the American Jewish front at a time that Israel needs more than the meek words, "We support Israel."

The applause line of "an undivided Jerusalem, the eternal capital of Israel" is now rarely used by our Jewish establishment leadership, although celebrated daily by the Jewish and Christian right who have it as part of their soul. We see that the status of Jerusalem as Israel's capital has even faced opposition from those we would have counted on previously. Israel now faces devastating security issues if it returns Judea and Samaria, and yet there continues to be a push for Israel to reach a peace that will not bring peace but would simply put Israel at greater risk with the Palestinians, who refuse to recognize Israel as a Jewish State and actually see Israelis as occupiers of the entirety of Israel. The American Jewish community has an extraordinary responsibility to Israel now, and silence is just not acceptable.

The fact is that today's Islamic world is looking to expand its influence and its beliefs throughout the world, and that includes sharia. In the most recent radical Islamic terrorist attack in Libya, resulting in the death of our American ambassador and three other members of our diplomatic corps, in what clearly was a premeditated terrorist killing, some Americans are so politically correct that they refuse to call it what it was. And that included the White House.

The attacks, and riots, were initially blamed on the anti-Muslim film clip on YouTube, and were not considered pre-meditated. There were calls for punishing those involved in the film and limiting or closing down its distribution. This is not the American way, and it is not the Jewish way. We must remain vigilant about limiting a traditional and cherished value of our U.S. Constitution, our freedom of expression. Too many are being apologists and making excuses for the Islamic radical actions against the U.S. Israelis have been facing this clash of civilizations for many years, and Americans are now seeing it firsthand.

The dangers of sharia include limitations on speech and free expression; extremely regressive treatment of women and the loss of women's rights, as we now see spreading in the Middle East; and the unification of church and state in government, with the rights of Christians and others being denied, and in the rules and laws of the State. You would think that the Jewish left would awaken and speak out, but instead, there is continued silence.

So, I call for a time of renewal in our Jewish community, fitting with this holiday season. A time of new responsibility. Review your long-held beliefs in light of the facts on the ground now, and not with wishful thinking based on your world of the past that you are holding on to. I call for a reevaluation of Jewish leadership, not leading from behind with a silence that is deafening, and an excuse, a charade based on consensus not being there. If you are in leadership at any level, it is not about taking the common position; it is about being unique and standing proudly forward at a time when you are called on to lead. It's a necessary time for greatness.

If you are not in an organizational position of leadership, you must remember that those who have transformed our Jewish history were not all in leadership positions, and when they stood up for our interests, they made a difference. Each one of us needs to go through that same process of reevaluation and renewal, and be courageous and bold, for each one of us is carrying the torch for our Jewish people in this generation, whether through our voice, message, actions or vote.

Abraham, Miriam, Joseph, Moses, Joshua, Esther and so many others of our Jewish ancestors acted on our behalf against the common thinking, showing courage and leadership, and they ultimately guaranteed our continuation as a living, vibrant Jewish people. Prime Minister Netanyahu is doing that for Israel today.

We cannot have less in America! So, I ask, who is the true leader in the American Jewish community today?

HOLDING ON TO OUR JEWISH HOMELAND: NO, YOU CANNOT TELL MY PEOPLE TO GO

January 2014

An interesting thing happened when I watched the movie, Mandela: Long Road to Freedom. I listened, and learned, and applied his thinking to Judea and Samaria. His concern was apartheid and that the powerful people in South Africa were directing the destiny of his people, and he asked the right question, "Am I to allow that powerful person to tell my people where to be!"

Well, I say the same thing, "Are we to allow the world powers to tell the Jewish people that they cannot live in their Biblical homeland, Judea and Samaria, and take away our rights to control our own destiny there? I say no on every level.

Let's really take a look. The Israel of today is a small sliver of land; one country carved out of the wide expanse of the former Ottoman Empire, with the Arabs being given the overwhelming bulk of the land for their numerous countries and kingdoms, including a country for the Palestinian people, Jordan. With the League of Nations unanimously declaring in 1920, "whereas recognition has been given to the historical connection of the Jewish people with Palestine, and to the grounds for reconstituting their national home in that country," and with the Balfour Declaration, the San Remo Conference and the Treaty of Sevres, the League of Nations, the U.N."'s declaration of statehood, and so many wars and treaties later, the issue of Israel's right to all the land that it now has reclaimed must be a closed issue.

As Churchill voiced it, the Jewish people returning to its land in Palestine are "further development of an existing community," and he added that it should be known that the Jewish people "are in Palestine as of right."

Fact: The Arabs refuse to recognize the right of the Jewish people to have even one state of their own, notwithstanding the reality of Israel as a leading country in the world. The Arabs want to destroy Israel, and the Jewish community wants it to continue to exist. That is the essence of the continuing problem. Israel has shrunk its land in the name of peace, sacrificing its rightful land – land it reclaimed in wars brought against it by the Arabs with the directed intention of destroying Israel, or as they term it, throwing Israel and the Jewish people back into the Sea.

Fact: With 700,000 Jewish people now living in Judea and Samaria, including post-1967 Jerusalem, the Jewish homeland is now being reconstituted in its ancient homeland after 2,000 years. Hebron, Beit-El, Shiloh, Shechem, and Bethlehem are all Jewish centers of great significance in our biblical history, and each continuing to thrive with Jewish people living on the land. Dani Dayan, chief foreign envoy of The Yesha Council, put it succinctly, "The Jewish communities of Judea and Samaria are not only legal but are impeccably legitimate. Shiloh in Samaria and Hebron in

Judea are the cradles of Jewish civilization, and as such the centers of the Jewish sovereignty, preceding even Jerusalem. These are the sites in which the ancient Jewish Tabernacle stood and where the founding fathers and mothers of the Jewish people were buried, where King David set up his first capital and where Jews have lived from time immemorial."

Now, let's take a realistic look at what will happen if this land would be handed over to the Palestinian Arabs as part of a supposed peace plan. First, all Jews would be forced to leave, be forced to march out of their sacred land and remove remnants of their current civilization there. In fact, if the withdrawals for peace with Egypt in the Sinai, and with the Palestinians in Gaza are a guide, not only will every Jewish person, house, synagogue, greenhouse and flower have to be removed, even every Jew who was buried there will have to have their graves moved out. Yes, all of that was required when Israel left Yamit and Sharm El Sheik in the Sinai, and Gush Katif in Gaza. We will never forget, and we cannot ever have that happen. Never again!

This is not just an Israeli issue. It affects all Jewish people, in Israel and in Diaspora, for after withdrawal the worldwide Jewish community can expect to never visit its sacred places again, as we would not be allowed back on the land. And there may not be another opportunity for future generations, as one could reasonably expect that the Palestinian Arabs, with control in their hands, will attempt to destroy each and every Jewish site in Judea and Samaria, to essentially eliminate all remnants of a Jewish civilization on that land. That's their way of ensuring an end to a Jewish future there, by destroying a Jewish past.

Well, world, that's not who we are. As a Jewish people, we will not stand by and let that happen. Jewish survival has always been based on forging ahead. Going back to the time of Moses, the Jewish people were not willing to remain as slaves, and a leader emerged to take us out. Whenever we have faith, and believe in a guiding hand, we forge ahead.

When Moses was told to lead his people into the Promised Land, Canaan, the Jewish people knew they would face battles from people who did not want them to live there. Yet they had faith and were victorious. In the multiple wars in Israel, with odds against the Jewish people, Israel won each time. Notwithstanding the Holocaust where the Europeans destroyed six million of our own, the Jewish people forged ahead when they may have collapsed, and now live in a golden age in our history, in Israel, in America, and throughout the Diaspora.

We have seen Jewish land and property taken away previously in Europe and in the Arab countries. So, is this a surprise? Not really. We have seen the removal of Jews from their territory previously in Europe and in the Arab countries. So, is this a surprise? Not really. We have seen worse previously from Europe and the Arab countries, threatening our very existence, so if they press for policies today that once again, though more subtly, threaten the very existence of Israel and the vibrancy of a Jewish civilization in Judea and Samaria, we should not be really surprised.

A great Jewish Zionist leader Ze'ev Jabotinsky, in the early 1900s took a tough stand when the British controlled the lands that were to be divided into the countries of the modern Middle East. He rightly stated that what comprised Judea, Samaria, Jerusalem and Israel was always Jewish land, and that any Arab claims on the land would simply be attempts to steal the land. So, it is time today for the Jews to surprise the world, and to say, in his words, "no, you cannot steal our land".

Let's be clear about the land in question. Israel has every right to each and every inch of that land, by historical and legal right.

It is outrageous that the world today should declare once again its position that Jews have no place in their ancestral homeland, and should essentially say, "get out."

Israel was attacked in 1967 and 1973, defended itself, and in the process was able to reclaim land that had been wrongfully taken from it: Judea, Samaria, and part of Jerusalem. Jordan controlled that land for years, although only two countries in the world had recognized their claim to it. In 1988. 10 years after Israel made a great sacrifice for peace by giving back nearly 50 percent of its land, Sinai, to Egypt, and in the midst of the first intifada by Arafat, the Jaffee Center for Strategic Studies issued a landmark report, "Israel's Options for Peace". Six options were given after much study, with a seventh recommendation forming the basis for the two-state solution.

The Jaffee Center Report called for defensible borders for Israel, and security arrangements, never calling for the return of all the land. It was the expectation that Israel would retain control of the Jordan Valley, and that Jews would remain in Judea and Samaria after the Palestinian state was established side-by-side with Israel. There would be demilitarization of the land, early warning and air-defense systems, a significant transition period for testing before any sovereignty was given up, and peace treaties in the works with other Arab countries. It was never intended, nor even contemplated, that Jews would entirely leave the land as part of the peace, for that's no peace at all.

Today, from the history of negotiations and current statements in the media, thinking exists that Israel should return to the 1967 land status, trade parts of its land if it wants to remain in any part of Judea and Samaria, force all Jews to remove themselves and their communities of generations, as well as IDF forces and outposts, even early-warning stations, and then have on the table discussion of the status of Jerusalem, and have the Temple Mount remain off limits to Jews. And of course, there's the issue of refugees.

This is insanity at best and relative suicide at worst. Changes since 1988 include the total withdrawal from Gush-Katif; the establishment of a Hamas-led Gaza with no Israeli controls; a Hezbullah power-center in Lebanon; turmoil and danger in Syria; Egypt continuing in a revolutionary swirl; and an enemy in Iran with its stated policy of eradicating Israel, and thousands upon thousands of missiles targeted for Israel, with the future potential of nuclear and chemical warheads.

So, when powerful people in the world see fit to cast their design on the future of the Jewish people, we have to say to them, "No, you cannot tell my people to give up our ancestral homeland that Israel reclaimed in wars defending their land, and that is my history and my legacy, and now guards the security perimeters required potentially for Israel's future existence." Whether the recent policy decisions on Iran prove right or wrong, we'll see in the future. What is now more eminently clear is that the case for remaining in Judea and Samaria became much stronger.

Forge ahead, the world Jewish community must, for this is the historic land of the entire Jewish people. So, we say to Israel, which is our front-line there, build communities today, and continue to rediscover our ancient communities lost for thousands of years. That must be the plan. I have called for the annexation of Judea and Samaria for years, and once again call on the Knesset and Prime Minister to make that choice. Do it in 2014, for Israel and for all the Jewish people in Diaspora.

The Palestinian Arabs can choose to remain in Judea and Samaria, a choice the Jewish people would not have if that land ever became a Palestinian state. The fact is that Jews and Arabs live together on that land today, and their economy is doing well, and the fact is they are living mostly at peace and mostly well. Yes, there are limitations today, and in a new situation of peace without leadership impediments, the future can be bright for all peoples on that land. So, forge ahead, Israel, and we will be with you.

Once again citing the words of Nelson Mandela from the four walls of his cell, as taken from President Obama's eulogy, "It matters not how strait the gate, how charged with punishments the scroll; I am the master of my fate, I am the captain of my soul!"

No, world, you cannot tell my People what to do with our land. The Jewish people's history and future are in Judea and Samaria. It is time to take a stand for our claim, our rights and our legacy, and it is time to do so now.

ABOUT THE AUTHOR
HOWARD TEICH

MY MISSION IS TO DREAM OF, AND CREATE A CONTEXT OF JUSTICE AND TOLERANCE, AND INSPIRE EVERYONE WITH A SPIRIT OF SPIRITUALITY AND EXCELLENCE.

As you review my biographical sketch, please keep in mind this Mission Statement that I drew up for myself probably twenty years ago. I mention it, as it has meaning for me as to the success of carrying out my value for me in living my life, for I see my life as a legacy instrument, one that will provide lessons for others, and service to the world. I point this out particularly for those who are young – being true to oneself in one's life is first prize, as I see it. -HT

Biographical Sketch

Howard Teich, president of The Howard Teich Network and a practicing New York attorney, has a wide-ranging background in business, civic, cultural, and social interests in the New York and national arena. He has chaired and served on a multitude of non-profit Boards of Directors and Advisors.

Among those are many in the Jewish world including Israel Bonds, Salute to Israel Parade, American Friends of Ariel University, New York Board of Rabbis, AJCongress, Jewish Community Relations Council of NY, NYC Jewish History and Heritage Map Project. Manhattan Jewish Historical Initiative (MJHI), Brooklyn Jewish Historical Initiative (BJHI), The Bronx Jewish Historical Initiative (BxJHI), and Project Interchange.

He has also served on such Boards as: Smithsonian's National Museum of the American Indian (NMAI – NY), Smithsonian's National Regional Council, Association on American Indian Affairs (AAIA), National Action Network (NAN), Soldiers', Sailors', Coast Guard and Airmen's Club of NYC, Ecuador's environmental organization Ecominga, All Stars Project, Manhattan Playhouse, 31 Council on Human Rights, Arts Horizons' Leroy Neiman Arts Center in Harlem, Boys Choir of Harlem, and National Task Force on Life Safety and the Handicapped.

He has been appointed to numerous positions over the years, including NYC Comptroller's rep to Wildlife Conservation Society (WCS), National Advisory Council (NAC) of the U.S. Small Business Administration, NYS Matrimonial Commission, Coalition on Judicial Justice, Mayor David Dinkin's Commission on Protocol, Alt. Delegate to the National Fire Protection Association's Safety to Life Committee, and Assoc of Bar of NYC's Committee on International Arms Control and Security Affairs.

He is Founding Chair of New Democratic Dimensions, has led NYS Citizens Committee efforts in Presidential and Gubernatorial campaigns, served as a Trustee of the New York State Democratic Committee, was a member of the Democratic National Committee's National Finance Council. and fundraises for local and national candidates. He initiated legislation in the House and Senate in the 1990s to create Democracy Day in America. He has appeared on radio and cable TV shows, serving as co-host of a weekly civic issues show in NYC for two years.

He received the "Robert Briscoe Award" from the Emerald Isle Immigration Society, 1999 Rev. Martin Luther King "Living the Dream" Award from Governor George Pataki, 2000 "Spirit of New York" Award from Councilwoman Una Clarke, 2001 "Jewish Heritage Award" from Brooklyn Borough President Howard Golden, 2008 "Bridge Building Award" from the All-Stars Project, and 2009 NYC City Council Jewish Heritage Award.

Mr. Teich lives in Manhattan, New York City. He graduated from Boston University School of Law (J.D.1970), the University of Pennsylvania (B.A.1967), and Huntington High School (1963). He is a three-time NYC marathon runner and finisher, and since 1999 he has been listed in editions of Who's Who in the East, Who's Who in America, and Who's Who in the World.

www.ingramcontent.com/pod-product-compliance
Lightning Source LLC
LaVergne TN
LVHW021537080426
835509LV00019B/2696